DREAM

RESORTS

DRE-AM

RESO

Andrea Chambers

R T S

25 Exclusive
and Unique
American Hotels,
Inns, Lodges
and Spas

Clarkson N. Potter, Inc./Publishers
DISTRIBUTED BY CROWN PUBLISHERS / NEW YORK

The author had made every effort to verify
all facts and descriptions in this book and to
make it as up-to-date as possible. However
changes in policy, management, standards,
and facilities may occur at any time.

The author has also attempted to credit all
historical references when available. Any
omissions or misattributions are inadvertent,
and any necessary corrections will be made in
future editions.

In some instances, the author has changed
the physical description, occupation, or
residence of guests to protect their privacy.

Copyright © 1983 by General Publishing
Company Limited

Published by Clarkson N. Potter, Inc.
One Park Avenue, New York 10016 and
simultaneously in Canada by General
Publishing Company Limited, 30 Lesmill
Road, Don Mills Ontario M3B2T6

Manufactured in Holland

Library of Congress Cataloging in Publication Data

Chambers, Andrea.
Dream resorts.

Bibliography: p.
Includes index.

1. Hotels, taverns, etc.—United States—Directories.
2. Resorts—United States—Directories. I. Title.
TX907.C53 1983   647'.9473   83-8242

ISBN: 0-517-54958-1

Designed by Two Twelve Associates

10 9 8 7 6 5 4 3 2 1
First Edition

To Bill and to my family

Contents

Acknowledgments   viii

Introduction   ix

The Northeast

Maine
1   *Black Point Inn*, Prouts Neck   2

New York
2   *The Point*, Upper Saranac Lake   9

The Midwest

Michigan
3   *The Grand Hotel*, Mackinac Island   17

The Southeast

Florida
4   *The Boca Raton Hotel and Club*, Boca Raton   25
5   *The Breakers*, Palm Beach   33

Georgia
6   *The Cloister*, Sea Island   41

Virginia
7   *The Homestead*, Hot Springs   49

West Virginia
8   *The Greenbrier*, White Sulphur Springs   57

The Southwest

Arizona
9   *The Arizona Biltmore*, Phoenix   65
10   *The Arizona Inn*, Tucson   73

Colorado
11   *The Broadmoor*, Colorado Springs   79
12   *Tall Timber*, Durango   86

New Mexico

13 *Inn of the Mountain Gods*, Mescalero   94

      Sante Fe   100

14 *The Bishop's Lodge*   102

15 *Rancho Encantado*   109

Texas

16 *The Mansion on Turtle Creek*, Dallas   117

Utah

17 *Deer Valley Resort*, Park City   124

The West Coast

California

18 *The Golden Door*, Escondido   132

19 *Ingleside Inn*, Palm Springs   141

20 *San Ysidro Ranch*, Montecito   149

21 *Sonoma Mission Inn*, Boyes Hot Springs   157

Oregon

22 *Salishan Lodge*, Gleneden Beach   166

Washington

23 *Rosario Resort*, Eastsound, Orcas Island   174

Hawaii

24 *Kapalua Bay Hotel*, Kapalua, Maui   181

25 *Mauna Kea Beach Hotel*, Kamuela, Hawaii   189

What It Costs   200

Bibliography   203

Sources   204

Photo Credits   205

Acknowledgments

Dream Resorts is an effort that required the advice and support of countless friends, colleagues, and members of the travel and hotel industries. In my year of traveling, I constantly encountered people who were willing to go far out of their way to show me around, share their knowledge, and direct me to local historians and experts. You know who you are and I am extremely grateful.

Special thanks to the travel consultants, educators in the field of hotel management, resort experts, and fellow travelers who guided me during the selection process. And also to:

The staffs of the hotels I visited for their willingness to spend long hours helping me learn about their resorts' history, facilities, and guests. The list of proprietors, resort staffers, and local experts who cooperated on the project is endless. I would like to especially thank: Virginia Graham at The Arizona Inn; Mark Weber and the Thorpe family at The Bishop's Lodge; Normand Dugas at The Black Point Inn; Sig Kaufmann at The Cloister; John Miiller at Deer Valley; Annharriet Buck and Rachel Caldwell at The Golden Door; Sharon Rowe and Robert Conte at The Greenbrier; John Gazzola, Jr., at The Homestead; Marilyn Baker at Ingleside Inn; Tommy Morel at Inn of the Mountain Gods; Carolyn Hunt Schoellkopf and Robert Zimmer at the Mansion on Turtle Creek; Colin Cameron and Christina Noah at Kapalua Bay Hotel; Betty and John Egan at Rancho Encantado; Russ Cleveland and Mary Arnstad at Salishan Lodge; Edward Safdie and Rebekah Conner at Sonoma Mission Inn.

The contributing photographers who showed such care and dedication.

Linda Marx, my research associate in Florida, and Bill Shaw in Washington for their many efforts and enthusiastic support.

Vicki von Gontard at Ports of Call and Mackey Arnstein at Mackey Travel for their excellent handling of my trips.

My agent, Amanda Urban, for her hard work and advice in getting this project under way and for her friendship and support through the long months.

Carol Southern and Michael Fragnito of my publisher, Clarkson N. Potter, Inc., as well as to Gael Dillon, and David Bauer for extending themselves far beyond limits.

My editor, Nancy Novogrod, a very special thanks for her unfailing enthusiasm and sound advice. Through weeks and weekends, she worked on copy and made suggestions as to content and style. Her good judgment and skills greatly influenced this book.

My husband, family, and friends, for understanding.

Introduction

America is rather like life. You can usually find in it what you look for. If you look for skyscrapers or cowboys or cocktail parties or gangsters or business connections or political problems or women's clubs, they will certainly be there. You can be very hot there or very cold. You can explore the America of your choice by plane or train, by hitch-hike or on foot. It will probably be interesting, and it is sure to be large.

E. M. Forster
Two Cheers for Democracy

Not only E. M. Forster, but other discerning Englishmen as well, such as Aldous Huxley, Lawrence Durrell, and Anthony Trollope, were fascinated by the vastness and variety of America. Its own citizens, however, have too often looked to Europe as the source of their richest travel experiences. But in recent years discriminating travelers have discovered America. This book is for those who have come to appreciate the culture, scenery, and vacation playgrounds of the United States, and for the uninitiated who are willing to give America a try.

But it is not just for any old traveler. The 25 resorts selected for inclusion in this book are exclusive, expensive, and unique. Most offer a full range of excellent recreational facilities on the premises or nearby. But they are not merely places to play golf or tennis or to lie on a beach. They are much more. *Dream Resorts* is for the traveler who believes that if he is going to invest time and money in a vacation, it should be in surroundings that are elegant, unusual, and even historic. Most of the resorts in this book have a past. Presidents have slept in their suites, famous authors have walked their grounds, the cream of Hollywood and high society has entertained in their salons. A trip through their corridors is a trip through a segment of America, past and present.

This book is a personal look at these resorts: what special features they have to offer, who goes to them, who runs them, and what tales their walls can tell. It is also the story of the people who created them and contributed to their success. Very often there is a single force behind the resorts, a man or woman who had a vision and the means to carry it out: architect Addison Mizner at

The Boca Raton Hotel and Club and at The Cloister; Laurance S. Rockefeller at Mauna Kea; John D. Gray at Salishan Lodge; Isabella Greenway at The Arizona Inn; Spencer Penrose at The Broadmoor; Carolyn Hunt Schoellkopf at The Mansion on Turtle Creek; actor Ronald Colman at San Ysidro Ranch, to name a few. Their entrepreneurial spirit is the same one that formed America.

In selecting these resorts, the aim was to provide a cross section of America's best. Not all are sweeping, grand-scale hotels. A few are intimate little places for those who like quiet hideaways. (They are *not*, however, country inns.) One, The Golden Door, is a strenuous, yet sybaritic health spa; another, the Sonoma Mission Inn, offers a spa program in a separate facility on the grounds. Yet another, The Mansion on Turtle Creek, is a city hotel with the cachet and ambience of an exclusive European pension. The majority are open year round; hence, they are clustered most heavily in the southern tier of the United States and in California and Hawaii. Some take in conferences because economically their massive size necessitates this. That doesn't mean, however, that there are hordes of conventioneers crowding the lobby, or that you can't find a deserted, romantic corner.

In reading this book, keep in mind that inevitably there are many omissions. Not every resort could be included. Some that are may undergo sudden shifts in management, services, and quality. That's the nature of the business, although I hope you will experience all as it should be. You may find yourself picked up at the airport in a Rolls-Royce, drinking champagne in your own private hot tub, and nibbling the hand-dipped chocolates left on your pillow before slipping under pure-cotton sheets. Go with high spirits and all your available cash and credit cards. Remember, as Ralph Waldo Emerson once said, "The world is his who has money to go over it."

DREAM

RESORTS

Black Point Inn

Prouts Neck, Maine

To the handful of old-timers, he is a distinct memory; an aloof, wiry little man impeccably dressed in tweeds and tam-o'-shanter, scampering over the rocks with his terrier, Sam.

But to most of the residents and visitors of Prouts Neck, Winslow Homer is the benefactor of a treasured legacy. Such masterpieces as *Cannon Rock*, *Fog Warning*, *Herring Net*, and *Driftwood* render a timeless testimonial to the assault of the Atlantic on the rocks of Prouts Neck. The spectacular cliffs and stunted, wind-bent trees of this small promontory captured the artist's imagination. He settled on the Neck in 1883 and lived there until his death in 1910.

This pocket of Winslow Homer country on the coast of southern Maine is still largely as he painted it. Over the years, the wild beauty of the area has attracted a coterie of devoted fans. The landed "Neckers," as they are sometimes called, are the members of an exclusive summer community that maintains its own private roads. But many others come to be pampered guests at the Black Point Inn. This Prouts Neck institution is almost—but not quite—as revered a landmark as the nearby cottage where the reclusive Homer did his work.

The B.P.I., as those who know call it, is one of those typically Down East structures of weathered brown-gray shingles and white trim. Generations of New Englanders have rocked in the moss-green wicker chairs on the wide porch that looks out to sea. They have taken brisks dips in the icy Maine waters, then scrambled ashore for chowder, broiled lobster, and hot blueberry pie in the restaurant. They have gone clamming on the beach, angled for bluefish on the rocks, and returned in time for a late-afternoon game of croquet by the rose garden. The pastimes are quiet, the trappings comfortably genteel, but not lavish. New Englanders, especially Down Easters, are a hardy sort who take pleasure in the joys of the simple life.

The guests at the quintessentially New England B.P.I. are definitely not looking for flash. They drive up in sensible Fords and Buicks (and an occasional Cadillac or Mercedes), sometimes toting a bicycle. Right away they sense the friendly unpretentiousness of the inn. By the front door is a bicycle rack, something a more snobbish hotel might scoff at. On the front lawn is a small bird cage. A picturesque, seven-sided cupola rises from the roof. (According to local legend, a mysterious Chinaman hanged himself up there many years ago.)

Parking their station wagons and their Raleigh bikes, the guests—blue-blooded Bostonians, mainline Philadelphians, and New Yorkers with the right social connections—unpack and get ready to settle in for a week, or maybe a

3

month. Some of the old-timers, who have been coming for as long as they can remember, ask the management to go up to the attic and pull out the straw hats and bathing outfits they stored there the summer before. Other guests slip into well-worn Topsiders, comfy crew-neck sweaters, and baggy pants. Here and there, legs tanned from long hours of tennis extend from linen Bermudas. In the evening, out come the white pants (green, too), navy blazers, and rep ties on the men and simple, tailored summer frocks on the women. The B.P.I. is *not* the kind of place where a woman would comfortably flash an impressive décolletage or show of diamonds. Besides, the lobster bibs (the hotel believes in serving the sweet Maine lobster at least once a day) might ruin the effect.

The management, in turn, maintains a due regard for the wants and traditions of the quietly affluent. Afternoon tea and cookies is an unswerving daily ritual, as is the serving of finger bowls after every meal. At the front desk, ask for change and you unfailingly will be handed crisp new bills. After all, the wealthy, it is said, don't like to handle dirty money.

Because unnecessary change, too, is often frowned upon in these circles, the inn is careful to maintain a status quo in its decor. The hotel dates back to 1878, when Prouts Neck (named after an early settler from Boston) was a quiet fishing village dotted with a few summer boardinghouses. Over the years, the Black Point Inn was lovingly nurtured by a series of gentlemen-owners. They decorated it with Queen Anne and Chippendale furniture and made certain that the wide-board pine floors were immaculately polished. The present owner is Normand Dugas, a hardworking hotelman from Hampton, New Hampshire.

Under Dugas's careful eye, the inn has been very subtly refurbished. Its lobby and parlors remain as practical and proper as your grandmother's sitting room. The sofas and chairs, freshly upholstered, are covered in those brocades and meticulous small prints New Englanders have loved since the *Mayflower* landed. In case you forget where you are, there is a wooden model of that venerable boat on the mantelpiece in the lobby. By the front door is an old doctor's scale, a traditional fixture in New England inns (presumably so that guests will weigh themselves periodically and not overindulge). Nearby, in the so-called Music Room, the grand piano stands where it has for as long as anyone can remember. The Queen Anne sofa is covered in soft green velvet, and the big wing chair by the window is done up in dusty rose and cream-colored flowers. Over in the cocktail lounge, which has always been called The Meeting Room, the leather club chairs are functional if not esthetically pleasing.

Upstairs in the inn, or in the various guests cottages, the rooms, by some standards, could use the sophisticated New York decorating hand of a Carleton Varney or a Sister Parish. But avoiding that kind of thing is what the B.P.I. is all about. The white crewel bedspreads, ruffled white curtains, rock maple beds,

and little Colonial print wall coverings are what you used to see in Nantucket or East Hampton before those places got so chic.

Guests seem to appreciate Dugas's respect for the past. "Prouts Neck is the most unchanged of any place I know," says Mrs. Marjorie Gardener, who first visited the Neck in 1904 and now spends every summer at the inn. The hotel has a rather venerated circle of white-haired ladies who return each summer. They gather for afternoon tea, and for after-dinner viewing in the television room. One evening a distinct clucking could be heard about the attire of a troupe of male ballet dancers. "Look at the undershirts they're wearing," sputtered one woman. She could not bring herself to even *mention* their tights.

Yet the inn also attracts a large contingent of families and prosperous young professionals, eager to swim, sail, play tennis, and absorb the uncommon beauty of the area. Occasionally, even movie stars have invaded the sedate world of the B.P.I. Paul Newman and Woody Allen, both retiring types, appeared to fit in. But when Elton John asked to stay at the inn during a concert in Portland, he was politely turned down. On another occasion, under a previous management, the governor of Connecticut was asked to leave The Meeting Room because he wasn't wearing a tie. "But I'm the governor of Connecticut," he protested. "You're *not* in Connecticut now," he was reminded.

The ethos of conservatism in these parts dates back to the seventeenth century, when stalwart, English colonists settled on the Neck. Black Point, as the area was then named after a local river, grew into an important trading and fishing center. But trouble was intensifying with the French in the area and with the Indian tribes. In 1690 the colonists were expelled from all the coastal settlements. In 1702 a second contingent of Englishmen set up a colony in Black Point. One autumn morning in 1713, a band of 20 townsmen out driving cattle was attacked by 200 Indians at Great Pond. A single survivor escaped. The pond, across from the golf course, is still called Massacre Pond.

By the late 1800s life was more civil on Prouts Neck. The fishermen and loggers were joined by the summer folk, who arrived by train and stage coach, sending their horses and coachmen ahead by boat. They whiled away the short Maine summers picnicking on the rocks (having "rock teas," as they called them) and riding horse-drawn hay wagons through the woods.

This was the bucolic scene that welcomed Winslow Homer. He found Maine more to his liking than the English seacoast where he had previously been painting. Homer settled in a small, green cottage he called "the factory." It stands today as a memorial, and visitors are welcome. Very often, Doris Homer, the widow of Winslow's nephew, Charles Lowell Homer, pops in and will gladly answer questions about the odd assortment of treasures: Homer's black rain hat hanging on the wall, his fishing nets, his paint box protected under glass, his collection of Shakespeare, and his tip-top deal table (the rest of his furnishings are largely gone). Homer liked to write on walls, and a few jottings remain. ("What a friend chance can be when he chooses" is one.)

Visiting the abode of the eccentric Homer is one way to pass an afternoon at Prouts Neck. Many visitors at the Black Point Inn also like to stroll the Cliff Walk high above the shoreline and form their own impressions of the ocean the artist so dramatically captured on his canvas. This narrow footpath meanders its way around the Neck and makes a pleasant two-hour walk. At each turn there is an alluring view: a tiny, private beach; spectacular boulders, their tidal pools heavy with sea grass and kelp; lobstermen hauling traps over the sides of their dories.

After the Cliff Walk, the stroller can head back to the inn for a restful rock on the porch. Or, he can venture farther in his wanderings. The Neck is really very small, some 130 acres, and can be easily explored. Its interior section is preserved as a bird sanctuary, traversed by paths and wooden walkways. This peaceful area once belonged to the Homer family, which gave the land to Prouts Neck. A plaque at one of the entrances to the sanctuary reads: "To Charles Savage Homer Jr., who gave these woods, and to Winslow, who through his brush, gave Prouts Neck to the world."

Back at the inn, it's almost teatime. A mother and her two daughters drift in from the Cliff Walk and pace in front of the tea table, awaiting the arrival of the cookies. Had they thought of it, they could have done as Neckers used to, and taken a picnic basket for one of those "rock teas." Instead, they finally grab a handful of confections and head out to the porch to watch the fading gold light and the gulls circling over the Atlantic. The father of the family joins them for tea, then settles down in a rocker to read the *Wall Street Journal*. His grandfather probably did the same at the B.P.I. Surveying the scene, Mrs. Gardener, a devotee of the area after 78 years, reports that people often ask her why she doesn't vacation anywhere else. "I've never even *tried* anywhere else," she says. "I never *wanted* to."

Prouts Neck, Maine   04074

Telephone

207-883-4311

On the Premises: Coastal Maine is known for its rocky promontories and picturesque coves, but not necessarily for its fine beaches. The Black Point Inn, however, manages to have all of the above. Where its heart-shaped sandy beach ends, jagged cliffs rise high above the surf. Beachcombing and clamming are splendid, but swimming is only for those who like a bracing dip. There is a large heated pool. The inn also has its own 39-foot Pearson sailboat for guests. At the nearby Prouts Neck Yacht Club, all kinds of sailboats can be rented for an excursion on the crests and swells of the Atlantic. Guest moorings are available for those arriving by yacht. The Prouts Neck Country Club, which is open to inn guests, has 14 tennis courts (10 clay, 4 all-weather), and an 18-hole golf course.

Rooms: The accommodations are spread out among the inn and three small cottages, two of which were constructed as vacation homes years ago by railroad barons. Each room is

A corner of the lobby.

slightly different in size and decor and has its own quaint charms. The older guests prefer the rooms in the main building because of their proximity to the dining room and lobby; families like the cottages, where individual rooms are grouped around a shared living room and pine-paneled library.

Meals: Codfish cakes, of course, are available on the breakfast menu, along with offerings such as hot cereal, eggs, pancakes, and homemade muffins. At lunchtime, if the weather is good, a hot and cold buffet is served by the pool. Steaming bowls of chowder and soup, and lasagna or chicken potpie might be the day's offering, along with hot dogs and hamburgers and salads of fruit, vegetables, chicken, and even lobster (Sundays only). Washed down with a Cape Cod Cooler (orange juice, cranberry juice, and vodka) or a blackberry sour, the meal easily holds one until tea and cookie time around 4:00. The dinner menu, which changes nightly, offers a five-course meal with New England and Continental accents. Some form of lobster (broiled, baked, boiled, or Newburg) is usually on the menu, unless it has been served at lunch. The German-born chef, Walter Beuttler, also prepares local delicacies like steamers and fried clam cakes. His more exotic offerings include venison with chanterelles, scampi de Jonghe, chicken Kiev, and sauerbraten. Beuttler's Fuerst Puëckler torte, a confection of sponge cake layered with liqueurs and topped with whipped cream, is a popular dessert, but so is plain old blueberry or apple pie.

Getting There: The Black Point Inn is about 8 miles south of Portland, which has a fairly large commercial airport. If driving north

7

from Boston, take the Maine Turnpike (Interstate 95) to exit 7; make a right turn toward Scarborough and Old Orchard Beach on Route 1; at the second traffic light, make a left turn onto Route 207 and continue 4.3 miles to the inn.

Money Matters: The hotel operates on the full American plan (three meals a day, plus afternoon tea and cookies). The cost per person, per day in a double room is $70 to $95, with suites slightly higher. The inn accepts MasterCard, Visa, and American Express.

Side Trips: The bird watching is good on nearby Stratton and Bluff islands; the Audubon Society organizes guided canoe tours (which can be arranged for at the inn). One might also want to visit Portland, a city that has enjoyed a renaissance in recent years, especially around the Old Port Exchange, which is now bustling with shops and restaurants. The Portland Art Museum has 18 new

8

Black Point Inn

Winslow Homers, donated by Charles S. Payson. Another attraction in the area is the headquarters of L.L. Bean in Freeport, about 20 minutes north of Portland. Open 24 hours a day, 365 days a year, this is the font for those down jackets and plaid shirts practical Down Easters have been wearing for as long as anyone can remember. Just to keep warm.

Observations: If you like whirlpool baths in your tub, lavish antique furnishings or zippy modern ones in your room, a dazzling lobby, and a chic East Side New York or Beverly Hills crowd, this is definitely not the place for you. The Black Point Inn is conservative and proper (some would say prim). Its reverence for tradition means that the furnishings are understated and the ambience staid. Many people, however, find a reassuring quality in all of this, a harking back to a time when the world was calmer.

2 *The Point*

Upper Saranac Lake, New York

In a land of towering conifers and ice-cold glacial lakes, Vanderbilts, Morgans, and Rockefellers once partied with an almost proud disdain for the harshness of nature around them.

Arriving via private railroad and stagecoach, they set up wilderness "camps" large enough for 100 and staffed by 50 or 60 servants. In this sylvan setting, servants inquired of guests whether they would like squab or perhaps cold filet mignon packed in their picnic baskets. Come evening, the band played, the crystal tinkled, and ladies in flowing gowns danced with their gentlemen beneath sloping, log-hewn roofs.

This was the Adirondacks during their heyday in the early twentieth century, an era before America's royalty discovered the watering holes of Europe. To this sparsely populated wilderness came such mainline Philadelphia families as the Biddles, Wisters, and Bodines, as well as New York financial giants like Adolph Lewison and John Loeb. Marjorie Merriweather Post, too, set up a 30-building outpost in the region and ordered local workmen to upholster her private fleet of mahogany runabouts in a soft, "Post" blue.

Today, the old families are mostly gone. The camps are closed. The Adirondacks are once again a preserve of simple North Country pleasures. Almost. On a promontory in the middle of Upper Saranac Lake, a well-bred entrepreneur named Edward (Ted) G. L. Carter is reviving the style and sensibilities of a bygone era. He is the proud owner of nine Paul Bunyan-style buildings constructed in the early 1930s for William Avery Rockefeller, a taciturn and reclusive nephew of John D. Rockefeller, Sr. Carter, who had spent many boyhood summers at his grandfather's camp in the Adirondacks, returned for a visit in 1979 after years of working as an international financier in Europe. Hearing that "Camp Wonundra," the old Rockefeller property, was on the market, he walked in, looked around, and said: "I must have it."

Soon, after extensive modernizing and redecorating, Carter began inviting friends and business associates for weekends. They sat lazily in front of the fire, or went cross-country skiing on trails traversed mainly by deer and snowshoe rabbits. One day a friend made an intriguing suggestion to his host: "Why not take in a few paying guests as they do in the grand houses of Europe?" Carter liked the notion of the "paying guest," or "P.G.," as the custom is known abroad, where the gentry sometimes find that this is the only way to pay the taxes or repair the roof on the quaint but crumbling family castle. To Carter, the idea seemed not only profitable, but entertaining: he would have an *endless* stream of guests.

One of the earliest P.G.'s at The Point was Prince Egon von Fürstenberg, a scion of European nobility and now a presence in the Manhattan fashion trade. "When I was a child in Europe," recalls Von Fürstenberg, "I remember my parents sending me to one of the Hapsburg castles in Austria as a paying guest. The Point was rather like that. Ted Carter knows how to make you feel very cozy and at home. He's a man of the world, and his home is a very nice one."

For those who have not frequented Hapsburg castles, vacationing at The Point requires a spirit of adventure and a willingness to toss out all preconceived notions about how to behave at a resort. Carter and his staff of 10 *do* carry luggage, serve fine gourmet meals, arrange recreational activities on request, turn down beds, and leave dainty chocolate-covered mints on the pillows. They *do not* offer a choice of menu at any meal except breakfast, provide room service, or outfit the quarters with televisions or telephones. Staying at The Point is rather like attending a private house party at a count's hideaway in the woods.

The host is duly selective. If callers seem overly concerned about the set menu or lack of room service, Carter may issue a telephone warning: "Hey, you might *hate* it here." If they carp about the prices (steep), he is not above harrumphing: "In *my* family, it's not considered polite to talk about money." In rare instances, he has offered a guest a refund and encouraged the person to

11

The back terrace of the main lodge.

The main lodge, with areas for lounging (*left*) and dining (*right*).

leave. The most celebrated case was a 65-year-old blonde woman of supposed royal ancestry who arrived in gold lamé pants and demanded: "Where is the disco? I left my three boyfriends at home, and I am here to meet men!" Eventually, quarters more to her liking were found in nearby Lake Placid.

Most guests, however, are hooked the moment they turn into The Point's private road, which meanders beneath tall balsams and hemlock trees. Arriving at the main lodge, a gabled structure of cedar and pine with casement windows imported from France, they step into an octagonal anteroom. Eight stern-faced reindeer stare at them from on high. The two eighteenth-century French gargoyles guarding the entrance to the 30 × 50-foot living room-dining room appear benign enough. Inside this massive hall, the vaulted ceiling seems to ascend forever. A fire crackles at each end of the room. Huge gray sofas, custom-made, invite the guest to settle in. Black lacquer coffee tables add a sophisticated touch, and Adirondack "twig" chairs convey a feeling of rusticity.

"Would you like a drink?" asks the host, gesturing toward an antique wagon that serves as a 24-hour open bar. "Some people are on the wagon. Here, we are *in* the wagon," he quips, eyeing his visitors for their response. All business once again, Carter shows his guests to their quarters and lets them know that lunch will be about 1:30, drinks in the waterside pub about 7:30, and dinner when it is ready. Carter will gladly explain, depending on the season, that the lake is fine for swimming and boating, and that 600 miles of accessible trails are available for cross-country skiing.

To the host's everlasting amusement, most people do none of this. They sit endlessly by the fire in the main lodge, or read quietly in one of the eight private rooms. Come mealtime, the guests sniff around the kitchen like hungry Adirondack black bears. When dinner is served, they all assemble at one big table. The host, impeccably attired in coat and tie, sets the unspoken dress code, and most guests comply. Women tend to wear dresses, and even long gowns on special party nights like New Year's Eve.

As the tapers burn down in Carter's Georgian silver candlesticks, his dinner partners address a three- or four-course feast that is meticulously planned. Car-

ter and his partner and executive chef, Jim Myhre, operate on the same entertainment principle used by a savvy hostess giving a dinner party: "Will everybody like it?" They do not serve liver, sweetbreads, or anything gamier than duck. Mostly, they stick to the basics — roasts, tournedos, sautéed fish and the like — beautifully sauced and garnished, and served on eighteenth-century Meissen china.

The atmosphere around the dinner table is as unpredictable as a mountain wind. On a given evening, a Houston oilman, who drove to The Point in his Rolls-Royce Silver Shadow, finds himself next to a Philadelphia socialite. A Nashville dermatologist turns inquiringly to the New York lawyer on his left. Soon they are discussing who has the bigger boat. "Everyone makes it quite clear at the beginning that they are sophisticated and successful," remarks a stockbroker's wife from Manhattan. "It's rather like dogs sniffing each other. Then it's forgotten."

On good nights, the talk moves easily, as it would at any self-respecting dinner party. Carter is delighted when diners argue good-naturedly about books or theater. "I love to have a *salon*," he smiles. On bad nights, and they do occur, guests can nod off, lulled by the endless supply of wine. Or, they may carry on in questionable taste. One summer evening a stag party of lawyers who had come up to go horseback riding at a nearby stable actually threw the tournedos around at dinner.

The host expects anything, from a touch of Mme de Staël's salon to the Mad Hatter's Tea Party. He diplomatically steers the conversation away from trouble spots. He also, when the mood hits him, plays raconteur. As a bon vivant and world traveler who has supped with the Duke and Duchess of Windsor and attended Queen Elizabeth's garden parties, Carter has endless stories to tell. He might also choose to talk about his illustrious relatives, like archaeologist Howard Carter, co-discoverer of King Tutankhamen's tomb in Egypt, or William Bradford, five-time governor of Plymouth colony. (Carter pays homage to Bradford each Thanksgiving by inviting a few Mohawks from a local tribe to share his turkey.) Or, Carter might mention financier Bernie Cornfeld, for whom he worked selling mutual funds before setting up his own shipping business, the Carter Container Company.

Now that he has left the high-pressured business world behind, Carter, better than most, appreciates the serenity of his mountain retreat. There is a timeless quality to the glacial lake and to the slender evergreens. Carter encourages his guests to drink deep. He purposefully does not keep newspapers at The Point. "Once, I considered ironing five-year-old copies of the *New York Times* and putting them outside people's doors in the morning," he recalls. "The news would have been more or less the same. After all, nothing changes."

Star Route
Saranac Lake, New York   12983

Telephone
518-891-5674

On the Premises: A resort like no other, The Point is essentially a private house party for paying guests. Millionaires and just-plain-folk come for the serenity in this eight-room retreat. For those who want sports, there is superb cross-country skiing (the management provides skis and boots). In summer the swimming and boating are fine on Upper Saranac Lake. The Point's flotilla includes a 32-foot barge with leather seats for cocktail cruises, a polished-mahogany Chris Craft (named "Boat of the Year" at the 1940 New York Boat Show), and "Diamond Lil," a shiny Glastron speedboat. There is also badminton, croquet, and a game room on the property; golf can be arranged at the nearby Saranac Inn Golf and Country Club.

Rooms: The large, individually decorated rooms, each with its own private bath, are spread out among the main lodge and several outer buildings. Almost all have fireplaces, huge closets, and spectacular views over the lake or across the Adirondack peaks. With names like "Iroquois," "Mohawk," and "Algonquin," the rooms are liberally accented by bold-colored fabrics with Indian-inspired motifs. Oriental rugs, English prints, and a variety of noteworthy antiques contribute to a mood of comfort and elegant simplicity. Perhaps the most luxurious accommodation is "Weatherwatch," an enormous suite with private porch, a massive fireplace of chiseled granite, and Carter family antiques. The smallest suite, "Trappers," has its own tiny dressing room and pine-paneled bath.

Meals: Only at breakfast is there a choice. Apple flapjacks, blueberry waffles, French toast, eggs, or virtually anything a guest wants will be served between 9:00 and 10:30 around the big kitchen table. Lunch, available in the main lodge in winter, and sometimes in a picnic basket in summer, is casual and imaginative: iced lemon soup and barbecued ribs one day, chicken braised in nuts and homemade apple pie with a slab of cheddar the next. The three-course dinners are classic. Chef Myhre has perfected dishes like rack of lamb with Provençal herbs, sole stuffed with salmon mousse, and fricassee of chicken with black currants. On those Thursdays when the lobsterman parks his refrigerator truck outside the Grand Union in the town of Saranac Lake, the chef buys fresh lobsters, splits them, fills the cavities with tomato fondue, and pours a white sauce over the tails. His best desserts include blueberry soufflé and gâteau Victoire.

Getting There: The Point is a six-hour drive from Manhattan on the New York Thruway to the Adirondack Northway (Route 87 north). Owner Carter, hoping to preserve the privacy of his property and discourage the curious, asks that specific driving instructions not be put in print. He urges guests to call him for exact directions before heading to The Point.

Money Matters: The price of a room at The Point includes three meals a day, wine at meals, and a round-the-clock open bar. The least expensive room is $200 per day; the others range in price from $250 to $450 per room. Credit cards are not accepted.

Side Trips: Artist Frederic Remington's birthplace is nearby, as is the cottage where Robert Louis Stevenson lived from 1887 to

15

1888. A house inhabited by abolitionist John Brown for a short time in the nineteenth century is also in the area. Lake Placid, site of the 1980 Olympics, is a short drive from The Point. There is downhill skiing at Big Tupper and Whiteface, both less than one hour away.

Observations: The Point is a unique vacation for people who do not demand the usual resort facilities, such as room service, television, and private telephones. It is not a place for couples who seek extreme privacy or meals alone. The companionship at lunch and dinner is the luck of the draw: the guests can be boring or fascinating, depending on their background, professions, and the mood of the moment. For the most part, however, travelers who search out a retreat like The Point are independent and adventurous sorts who are good company.

Weatherwatch (*left*) and Evensong (*below*) are the names of two of the guest rooms.

3 *The Grand Hotel*

Mackinac Island, Michigan

Christopher Reeve, in the guise of a talented young playwright of 1980, falls in love with an old photograph of a beautiful stage star, circa 1912. To the soaring notes of Rachmaninoff, he successfully wills himself back to the turn of the century. A heated romance follows as the actress, played by Jane Seymour, succumbs to his charms. Critics panned the movie *Somewhere in Time*, but praised the backdrop: The Grand Hotel.

If time does not exactly move backward at The Grand, it certainly does not rush forward. This improbable white leviathan, nearly 100 years old, is the pride of a small lilac-covered island in Michigan's Straits of Mackinac. Surrounded by the oceanic vastness of Lakes Huron and Michigan, it is a dot of wooded land rising, humplike, from the water. Prehistoric Indians, paddling toward its rocky shore, named the island Michilimackinac: great turtle. The abbreviated version, shortened sometime in the nineteenth century, is pronounced "Mack-i-naw" by the locals.

Newcomers arrive on Mackinac by ferryboat from the mainland, or by small plane. From that point on, all traces of modern transportation disappear. At the dock waits a horse-drawn carriage with a liveried driver, or a more plebeian buggy. The island fathers, you see, have banned automobiles since 1896, shortly after they were developed. With its civilized absence of engines, Mackinac Island is suspended, far more effectively than the movie, somewhere in time.

To the island's 600 year-round residents, the gentle clip-clop of horse hooves on the narrow streets is as much a part of the background as the sound of automobile horns are to city dwellers. But to visitors, the bustling carriage traffic is both quaint and a touch surreal. Horses haul garbage trucks, supply drays, and even pull a special taxi for the handicapped. In their wake, a fleet of men in yellow overalls and broad-brimmed hats scoop up the droppings in an energetic effort to keep the island clean.

As the horses plod past turn-of-the-century summer "cottages" with Victorian turrets and gingerbread trim, bicyclists weave in and out of their path. Horses, supposedly, have the right of way. Yet anything goes on the roadways that crisscross the island, 2 miles across at its widest point and 3 miles long. The cyclists are often fueled by the calories of the island's best-known souvenir, fudge. Even the old-timers aren't quite sure how Huron Street, the main drag, became lined with confectioners' shops selling banana, pistachio, mint, cherry, and all kinds of chocolate fudge. But one thing is clear: only the most strong-

willed can resist the aromas that billow out the doorways of the fudge kitchens and mingle, harmoniously, with the scent of lilacs and manure. The candy is a special lure to the day-trippers, who come over en masse on the ferry and are known, appropriately, as Fudgies.

The Grand Hotel stands coolly apart from all this pleasant madness, a proud clapboard palace on a hill overlooking the water. The approach is via a stately incline lined with Norway maples. They call it "Grand Hill," and no one questions why. At the top, eight United States flags and a phalanx of the hotel's mustard yellow and red ones snap in the breeze on The Grand's roof and project smartly from its balconies. On the colonnaded front porch, mustard yellow awnings shade the matching honeybee marigolds in the window boxes. Potted geraniums, the hotel's symbol since its opening in 1887, are everywhere. A line of white wicker chairs stretches up and down the 880-foot veranda. On a nice day, the porch is packed with guests doing needlepoint, writing letters, reading, or just plain staring at the blue of the water stretching as far as the eye can see.

Inside the lobby, the sounds are the notes of "Oklahoma!" and "Tea for Two." It happens to be afternoon teatime, and the pianist and violinist in white dinner jackets are playing their usual medley. By the Chinese Chippendale table, in front of the George III breakfront, a waitress arranges champagne, sherry, and tea. A passing parade of guests in casual skirts, shorts, or madras pants, and pastel jerseys gives their orders before settling down in one of the peach wing chairs or blue club chairs. A waiter in a black dinner jacket brings them their requested drinks and a tray of finger sandwiches filled with cucumbers and salmon mousse. A desk clerk rushes up and down with a little bell and a sign reading "Mr. Williams." This serves as The Grand's paging system, infinitely more genteel than a loudspeaker. Yet, there seems to be nothing improper about putting up a sign reading: "Dow Jones up 21 points. 110 million shares traded."

All over the hotel there are minglings of present and past. An errant golf ball bounces onto the road and gets crushed by a horse's hoof. In the forest green

The Grand Hotel

lounge, more like a gentlemen's club than a bar, a harpist plays while a group of computer experts discuss software. In the downstairs lobby, old newsclips and historic photographs of the hotel line a corridor that leads to a game room; there, teenagers are mesmerized by video games.

The guests, a mixture of old-timers who have been coming to Mackinac Island for years, as well as families and conference groups, are largely from the Midwest. They come for the lazy summer days and the pure, pollen-free North Michigan air, for the serpentine swimming pool at the edge of a great green lawn, for the golf and the tennis. But most of all, they come for the blend of island quaintness and sophisticated elegance one experiences at The Grand.

The man responsible for the hotel's new panache is Carleton Varney, the New York decorator. Varney, who had a love of breezy summer places from his childhood on the island of Nahant, Massachusetts, was hired by the management in 1978 to give the hotel a fresh new look while retaining its flavor. He started with the lobby, which was predominantly red with a garish red and gray carpet. "It was pure Roxy Theater," recalls Varney. He quickly transformed it into a gracious expanse of armchairs, tufted-velvet sofas, and a black, green, and red rug embellished with geraniums. "I tried to set everything against green walls to bring out the sea and the sky and the white feeling of the island," Varney explains. For the same reason, he had the ceiling painted a soft

"Thomas Jefferson" blue. Varney also highlighted the room with antiques, including the Chippendale tea table, a George II horsehair bench, a George III sideboard, and an Italian Directoire settee (circa 1790).

From the lobby, known as the parlor, Varney proceeded to the rest of the hotel. In the tea shop in the lower lobby, the wares are displayed in an antique cabinet originally used for grains. The authentic model of a Mississippi riverboat lights up inside, a source of pleasure to the mothers and children snacking on pastries and hot cherry or cold peppermint tea. (The hotel was so pleased with the decor that they named it Carleton's Tea Shop.) Another point of pride for Varney is the Audubon Bar, a handsome preserve where the walls are lined with Audubon prints and the lamps are fashioned from riding boots. The antique wooden decoys and the hunt pattern on the upholstery fabric heighten the feeling that one has dropped into an English club.

In his renovation of the guest rooms, Varney confronted layouts designed in the days when guests arrived with an entourage of maids and valets. The rooms overlooking the water were intended for the masters and mistresses; the much smaller ones on the back were for the servants. To give the whole place an airy feeling and to open up the smaller rooms, he selected whimsical stripes and prints for the wall coverings, and casual wicker and wood furnishings. In two cases Varney indulged his passion for history: the Lincoln Bedroom is closely modeled on the original in the White House; the Madison Room is a replica of an eighteenth-century bedroom done in the damask fabrics and peach colors that Dolley Madison loved.

To preside over the cuisine presented in Varney's splashy canary yellow, orange, and green dining room, the management chose Austrian-born Hermann Schwaiger. Chef Schwaiger's task was to lighten the cuisine. He did away with the steamed finnan haddie, the pot roasts, and the heavy stroganoffs, and added chilled summer soups and light veal and fish entrees. The famed Mackinac Island whitefish remains on the menu, and is as popular as it was when tourists first discovered the island.

The popularity of Mackinac Island as a civilized northern outpost for the smart set was prophesized by the American poet William Cullen Bryant as early as 1846. In his *Letters of a Traveler*, he wrote of his visit to the island and its potential as a tourist spot: "I cannot see how it is to escape this destiny. . . . The world has not many islands so beautiful as Mackinac."

Nor, noted other observers, so potentially commercial. Francis B. Stockbridge, a Michigan businessman and later a U.S. senator, saw the value of a major resort hotel on Mackinac and selected a plot of land on the island's west bluffs. He then induced three transportation companies serving the island—the Michigan Central Railroad, the Grand Rapids and Indiana Railroad, and the

Detroit and Cleveland Navigation Company—to join forces in building a colonnaded masterpiece overlooking the Straits of Mackinac. The companies, each taking a one-third interest in the project, were obviously hopeful that the magnet of a Mackinac resort would lure more passengers to their boats and trains.

From the outset in 1887, the resort set a standard of elegance. Built in an era of Victorian excess, The Grand was noteworthy for its uncluttered exterior. No cupolas, filigree, or elaborate fretwork were to be seen. The five-story sweep of Michigan white pine stretched across the bluff like an ocean liner. Over the years a series of skippers captained this ship. From 1923 until 1979, the owner was W. Stewart Woodfill, an Indiana man who had worked at the hotel as a desk clerk and manager before becoming the proprietor. Woodfill presided over his "little boardinghouse," as he sometimes called it, with a flair for hospitality and public relations. He plunked a sign on the porch reading: "This is the purest air in the world," and dared anyone to dispute him. He lured important politicians to his shores by offering them elaborate quarters in special suites designated for the "President" and for the "Governor of the State of Michigan." In the forties, he even leaked word to the press that Greta Garbo and Clark Gable were coming to The Grand Hotel. He then hired a young woman roughly Garbo's size to ride about, veiled, in a carriage. The island—and the press—were so intrigued about "Garbo" that no one bothered to ask what had happened to the missing Gable. After Woodfill retired to Arizona, the hotel came under the ownership of his nephew, R. Daniel Musser, Jr., a native Ohioan who also worked his way up the ranks at The Grand. Today, he presides over one of the few family-owned resorts in America.

The hotel, in turn, presides over an island where the past seems more real than the present. It is a place where the locals invite one another to ice-cream socials on the front porch and participate enthusiastically in stone-skipping contests on a windswept point. The fur-trading headquarters of John Jacob Astor on Market Street closed, it seems, only yesterday. The sound of musket-firing demonstrations at Fort Mackinac is more appropriate, somehow, than the hum of planes heading for the small island airport.

At The Grand, some traces of the past have, of course, disappeared. No longer does the hotel stage an annual track-and-field day, as it did in 1894. There are no spirited "gentlemen's rowing races," "bellboys' tub races," "greased pole events" (a $5 bill was placed at the end of a 25-foot pole extended over the water), or "egg races," during which riders trotted around a track holding an egg in a spoon. However, each August the hotel is the site of a World Sauntering contest. The goal is to get from one side of the long front porch to the other as slowly as possible—a metaphor, some might say, for the passage of time on this charmingly out-of-step island.

Mackinac Island, Michigan   49757

Telephone
906-847-3331

On the Premises: Perched on a bluff 100 feet above the Straits of Mackinac, The Grand Hotel offers a spectacular view of the Great Lakes and the soaring Mackinac Bridge that connects Michigan's Upper and Lower peninsulas. One could spend all day sitting on the front porch gazing at the scenery, and some people do. The hotel also has sporting diversions: a nine-hole golf course; four clay tennis courts, a huge, serpent-shaped pool with sauna; hiking trails; an exercise trail; horseback riding nearby; and bicycles for rent. Beaches on the island are small and rocky; the water is cold but swimmable.

Rooms: The rambling hotel has 226 rooms and 2 suites, each of which is different. Ask for waterfront accommodations that have already been redecorated by Carleton Varney. (The whole hotel is in the process of gradual renovation.) Varney loves bold colors and white wicker and wood furniture, which make virtually any one of his creations a visual pleasure. He might place a pink quilted comforter over a blue, pink, and green flowered dust ruffle in one room, and use purple stripes in the next. The baths are papered with the likes of tulips and trellises. If possible, reserve a room with a porch so that you can better watch the water and listen to the rhythmic clip-clop of the horses' hooves.

Meals: Wheat cakes with Michigan maple syrup are a good way to start the day at The Grand. Hot cereal, eggs, and freshly baked banana and blueberry muffins are also available. At lunch, a long buffet table is covered from one end to the other with cold salads, melons, cheeses, marinated vegetables and hot entrees such as Chinese chicken, shrimp creole, and corned beef and cabbage. The multicourse dinner menus offer continental selections: breast of chicken Orly, veal Marsala, seafood en croute, and rack of lamb, for example. The famous Mackinac Island whitefish is always on the menu. The "Grand pecan ball," a baseball-size scoop of French vanilla ice cream rolled in chopped pecans and topped with sinfully rich fudge sauce, is the favorite dessert; banana-cream pie and The Grand's cheesecake are also popular.

Getting There: Remember that The Grand is on an island that bans automobiles. Drivers must leave their cars in either St. Ignace on the Upper Peninsula or Mackinaw City on the Lower (special parking lots are provided). From there, they climb on one of the ferryboats that ply the straits for the ride of approximately a half-hour to Mackinac Island. At the island docks, The Grand's carriage is waiting. The nearest commercial airport is in Pellston, Michigan, about a half-hour by limousine from the Mackinaw City docks (the limousines are generally waiting to transport passengers to the ferry). Those who

23

The stately lobby, or "parlor."

sobriquet "Newport of the North" because of its grand Victorian "cottages" that dot the bluffs. Days could be spent on a bicycle exploring the roads and paths that wind along the limestone cliffs and into the wooded interior. In the downtown area, visitors can tour the old fur-trading headquarters, as well as an early blacksmith shop, and the "Indian dormitory" erected by the government for the local Indians after they gave up their rights to the land. A major highlight of the island is Fort Mackinac, built by the British, who considered Mackinac Island a strategic stronghold for their territory in the Great Lakes. Costumed guides take visitors through the blockhouse, gun platforms, and barracks; cannon salutes and musket-firing demonstrations are part of the display.

prefer to fly directly to the small airstrip on the island can arrange for an air taxi in Pellston or St. Ignace.

Money Matters: The Grand operates on the modified American plan (breakfast and dinner) and tosses in an after-dinner demitasse and snack. (There is an additional charge for the afternoon tea service.) The rate per person, per day in a double room ranges from $82.50 to $110. Tipping is not allowed. Instead, the management adds a standard surcharge of 18 percent to the daily room rate. Credit cards are not accepted; however, the hotel welcomes personal checks.

Side Trips: Mackinac Island has earned the

Observations: In the midst of a busy summer season, The Grand is a bustling place, and not for those looking for a quiet little hideaway. Families, members of conference groups, and curious visitors (who now pay an admission fee because too many nonguests used to crowd the premises) mill about in the lobby. If everybody decides to descend to the dining room at the same hour, things can get hectic. For the most part, however, the hotel is adept at handling large numbers of people, especially at crucial check-in and check-out times. The desk clerks and bellboys, many of whom are Michigan college students, are unfailingly cheerful and polite.

4 *The Boca Raton Hotel and Club*

Boca Raton, Florida

25

O nce there were pineapple patches, marshes, and eggshell white beaches deserted except for driftwood and washed-up cargo from shipwrecks. No Jaguars and Alfa Romeo convertibles cruised the dusty roadways. No sailboats painted pistachio green and passion-fruit pink ruffled the serenity of the waters. The residents, a hardy stock of planters, dined not on caviar and champagne, but on wild game and sea turtle. Then, two peripatetic strangers landed on Boca Raton's shores one perfect sunny day and turned a farm town into a palmy paradise. Addison and Wilson Mizner, one an eccentric architect, the other a reasonably successful playwright, had mined gold in the Klondike early on in their lives. Applying a Midas touch to Boca Raton, the Mizners, particularly Addison, transformed the steamy backwater into what some folks insist is the capital of the famed Florida Gold Coast.

26

**The Boca Raton
Hotel and Club**

Boca Raton today is snob-years removed from the ancien régime of Palm Beach. It is an incubator for the newly wealthy, who appreciate its manicured casualness and social willingness to accept almost anyone. In its Spanish-style stucco mansions and newer California contemporary "cottages" (some going for $2 million) live transplants from everywhere. Somehow, they seem to manage to do all their business by telephone. Of Boca Raton's 60,000 citizens, some 12,000 are said to be millionaires. Discriminating sorts, they are understandably concerned that Boca's growth and aesthetic values be carefully protected. Signs are limited in size and height, parking lots hidden behind hedges, and backyard waterways meticulously patroled.

In the midst of all this sensible splendor stands a hotel pink as a baby's bunting and palatial as the Spanish castles that danced in the architect's head. Addison Mizner, a man so unconventional that he sometimes shopped in his dressing gown, built the original Mediterranean core of the hotel, once called the Cloister Inn. The modern, 26-story Tower just south of the old inn, and the 7-story, 212-room Boca Beach Club to the east were added long after Addison had retired to Palm Beach. (During his final illness in 1933, Wilson wired him from Hollywood: "Stop dying. Am trying to write a comedy.")

The legacy left by Addison is pure drama. In fact, Frank Lloyd Wright himself is said to have expressed a grudging approval of Mizner's work, but added that he was no more than a set designer. Approaching Addison's stage, one drives beneath royal palms and past a gatehouse. The red-tiled roofs of the old Cloister rise from the shores of Lake Boca. Entering the lobby is like stepping into a European villa. In Gothic archway after archway, hammered-copper chandeliers sway slightly when the breeze picks up. They cast a mellow light on the purple and blue stained-glass windows and the gold and ruby-hued carpets. Everywhere one looks there are vestiges of the systematic buying trips Mizner took through impoverished parishes and cash-needy universities of Central America and Spain. Beneath the carved wooden beams stands a seventeenth-century credenza, a vestry settee, antique oak writing desks, and a refectory table.

In one corner of the lobby, some of the more esoteric objects acquired by Mizner in his rovings are assembled in a small museum. The visitor can peruse a fifteenth-century Renaissance monk's chair and Spanish "scissor" chairs (the forerunners of today's folding ones). Wrought-iron lamps, silver tureens, wine coolers, even a meat warmer from the hotel's earliest days, are on display, as are seventeenth-century English pin dishes used in the original Cloister bedrooms.

The hotel's various loggias, lounges, and salons offer more surprises. A mirrored foyer is lit by a fireplace and the blazing light of a crystal chandelier, a little like a court room at Versailles. Nearby, in the Patio Royale, one of the most popular restaurants, marble columns and arches stand out against walls the color of Florida coral. As the name implies, this was once a patio with a retractable ceiling; the effect is maintained with a small forest of lighted trees. In the adjacent Cathedral Dining Room, the walls are hung with tapestries. The

The Boca Raton Hotel and Club

14-carat gold-leaf columns rise toward the vaulted ceiling. But don't forget to look out the windows at the shimmer of the yachts cruising up and down the Intracoastal Waterway.

Down by the dock, a sleek, 43½-foot powerboat with teak and brass trim is waiting. This is *Mizner's Dream*, which provides shuttle service between the old portion of the hotel and the Boca Beach Club. Both a captain and a co-captain are on board to see that the seven-minute passage goes smoothly.

Arriving at the Beach Club, the visitor is effectively on another continent. The club, built in 1980, is a $22 million tribute to high gloss on the Gold Coast. "Would you care for a mimosa?" asks the young desk clerk as you check in. Soon, a complimentary glass filled with champagne, orange juice and Triple Sec is in your hand. Sipping it, you look around the rather modern lobby furnished in the burnished colors of fall leaves. A piano stands at one end, a red wicker bar (the source of the mimosa and other liquid refreshments) at the other. Outside, on the grassy knoll that separates the pink club from the blue ocean, there is a metal sculpture of a young man staring dreamily out to sea.

Real-life bathers hurry by. The Boca is one of those places where people do more than lie in poolside chaises and drink various concoctions of coconut milk, pineapple, and alcohol. At The Boca, they aggressively rent surfboards, sailboats, snorkeling gear, even canvas rafts. They take fishing seriously and go out on nocturnal forays for swordfish. They also golf long and hard on the course adjacent to the hotel before rewarding themselves at the 19th hole. (A few even eschew the pink-and-blue-striped golf carts.) Tennis players emerge dripping from the courts, then go for a swim. In the late afternoon or early morning, joggers pound the roadways or the hotel's special track.

They do all of this in style. Boca guests, notably the Beach Club crowd, are often hardworking professional types who enjoy the trappings of success. Although they don't necessarily flaunt flashy jewels or haute couture clothes, they do appear in Cartier watches, Gucci loafers, Ferragamo bags, and beautifully cut slacks, shorts, tennis outfits, and velour jogging suits. This isn't to say that *everyone* at the Beach Club is tanned, trim, and California chic. But the bejeweled women in long gowns and the gentlemen in tuxedos who frequent the dining rooms of the Breakers in Palm Beach do not, generally, gravitate to the Beach Club. The guests sipping Perrier (served in fluted champagne glasses) or white wine in the Cathedral Dining Room are fairly casual: light linen suits or blazers and slacks on the men; printed summer dresses, even jump suits and pants outfits for the women.

The cosmopolitan, but casual, clientele in this restaurant might have rankled The Boca's creator, Addison Mizner. He perhaps would have been astounded to see the modern Tower and Beach Club flanking his original, romantic inn. The "Michelangelo of architecture," as Mizner was once called, had envisioned an entire European-style city springing up out of the marshes and pineapple patches. It would have Spanish-inspired architecture, grassy parks, and rolling golf courses. It would be filled with learning institutions and libraries, and populated by millionaires. A magazine once called Mizner's idea for Boca Raton "a happy combination of Venice and heaven, Florida and Toledo, with a little Greco-Roman glory thrown in."

Certainly, the Florida of Mizner's era inspired grandiosity. "The famous Florida climate had become a kind of loony gas," wrote Alva Johnston in *The New Yorker*. "Subdividers hired poets to write odes in their honor. Shoestring operators named cities after themselves. The Mizners lost their sense of humor for a while, becoming Napoleons—Addison the Corsican of city planners, and Wilson the Bonaparte of finance."

Addison and Wilson displayed the first phase of their handiwork on February 6, 1926, the Cloister's opening night. The royal court that evening included author Theodore Dreiser, showman Florenz Ziegfeld, entertainer Al Jolson, socialite Mrs. Vincent Astor, and many more of her ilk, if not rank. Throughout the first Cloister season, the festivities were so lavish that old newsclips describe parties and steak roasts on the beach "with flames so high that passing steamers sent concerned messages inquiring of possible holocaust."

Then, in the summer of 1926, Mizner's Boca bubble burst. The land boom had gone bust all over Florida, and Boca Raton was no exception. The Cloister Inn, which had been managed by the Ritz Carlton Hotel, passed into the hands of creditors. Finally, in 1928, a rescuer arrived. Clarence H. Geist, a onetime railway brakeman from Indiana who had made a fortune in utilities, paid $1 million for the hotel. He poured another $8 million into developing the property into an exclusive club. Geist, a rough-hewn, uninhibited man who was known to run through the hotel lobby in his bathrobe, had lavish tastes. He hired the New York firm of Schultze & Weaver (Leonard Schultze was the architect for The Breakers in Palm Beach) to add 300 guest rooms, 5 patios, 2 swimming pools, a spa, a wide terrace for rocking chairs, a special dining room for children, and another for maids and chauffeurs.

After Geist's death in 1938, the hotel was owned by a succession of proprietors, including the U.S. government, which used it during the war years as rather posh barracks. In 1956 Arthur Vining Davis, an octogenarian aluminum tycoon, purchased The Boca. Davis, one of the founders of Alcoa, created the Arvida Corporation (an acronym of his name), which today owns The Boca Raton Hotel and Club, as well as a significant portion of Boca Raton proper. Davis continued to expand and develop the hotel, a practice Arvida has followed since his death. (In 1983, the hotel was sold to VMS Realty Partners, a Chicago-based real estate and holding company.)

The modern-day Boca has its share of guests who remember a long-gone era. "People marry here. They come back with their parents and their children," says George Roy, the general manager. "It's a way of life." Two couples who met at The Boca 38 years ago still get together there almost every winter. "It's our home away from home," comments a woman from New Jersey who comes every year with her husband and children and stays for seven weeks.

A passing parade of flashier guests also drops in at The Boca. A Saudi sheik paid an estimated $19,000 for virtually all of the stock in one of the hotel's boutiques. He had it sent up to his room for his wife, who didn't want to go downstairs. Frank Sinatra, Robert Merrill, and Mike Douglas have all played golf on The Boca course, redesigned in 1956 by Robert Trent Jones. Gerald Ford stayed for two weeks, and Robert Redford, Billy Graham, Bill Cosby, Shirley Temple, Polly Bergen, and even Elizabeth Taylor have visited The Boca. (Liz, however, bunked on a yacht docked in the marina.)

They come for the sun and for a prized spot on the Florida Gold Coast. Ironically, years ago the pirate Blackbeard was said to have frequented Boca Raton's waters and stashed his silver and gold booty in its sands. A few pieces of eight have actually been found. Perhaps the biggest treasure unearthed, according to local journalist Henry Kinney, was in 1925 when Addison Mizner's inventive brother Wilson secretly buried some doubloons. He had them "discovered," reports Kinney, "amid wild excitement among the land speculators." Today, a far savvier crowd knows that what really shimmers in these parts is the Cartier watches and the sunlight dancing on the graceful prow of a yacht.

501 East Camino Real
Boca Raton, Florida   33432

Telephone
305-395-3000

On the Premises: The Boca is a large, self-contained resort with 922 rooms, including 31 suites and 106 golf villas. The Boca Beach Club has 127 waterside cabanas, some equipped with wet bars. The recreational choices are particularly impressive. Besides the hotel's 18-hole championship golf course, there are 72 more holes at Boca West, a planned golf and tennis community owned by the Arvida Corporation and open to Boca guests. Australian tennis pro Warren Woodcock oversees the 22 clay-topped courts, 4 of which are lighted for night play. Water sports include swimming in four different pools, sailing, snorkeling, scuba diving, and deep-sea fishing. There is also a health club, a jogging and exercise track, volleyball, basketball, and badminton.

Rooms: In choosing where to stay at The Boca, determine whether you want the old-fashioned, European-style feel of the Cloister of the more modern comforts of the Beach Club or Tower. No matter where you stay, expect to find color television, direct-dial telephone, wall safes, and a Godiva chocolate on the pillow when you retire at night. (Many of the rooms also have mini-bars stocked with wine, Perrier, and 36 little bottles of booze.) In the new Beach Club, where the rooms are casually furnished in wicker and rattan, pastel-print fabrics, and abstract art, the sheets are 100 percent cotton and specially dyed a tiger-lily color. His and her terry robes hang in the bath.

Meals: An espresso bar, a beachside grill, and assorted lounges and very elegant restaurants give guests a wide choice. The Patio Royale and Cathedral Dining Room in the old Cloister section of the hotel are popular for breakfast and dinner. The Cabana restaurant at the Beach Club offers a superb view of the water and a lavish luncheon buffet. Another favorite at the Beach Club is the Shell Dining Room, a sophisticated salon decorated in shades of champagne and peach; the Continental cuisine is served on Fitz & Floyd shell-patterned china. Throughout the various dining areas, the menus offer classic French and Continental dishes, such as marinated saddle of venison with morels, roast duck with Calvados, sliced tenderloin stuffed with pâté, and Florida pompano and red snapper.

Getting There: The nearest commercial airports are in Fort Lauderdale and West Palm Beach, both about 30 minutes from the hotel. If driving to The Boca on Interstate 95, get off at Palmetto Park Road and head east to Federal Highway; continue south on the highway to Camino Real; go east on Camino Real to the hotel entrance, which is on the west side of the Intracoastal Waterway.

31

Money Matters: Most guests at The Boca are on the modified American plan (a full American plan is available, as is a European plan). On the MAP in high season (January to May 1) a double ranges from $205 per room in the Cloister to $315 in the Beach Club; suites range from $305 to $450. Summer rates at The Boca drop to less than half the high-season rates. The Boca accepts Master-Card, Visa, American Express, Carte Blanche, and Diners Club.

Side Trips: The community of Boca Raton, with its palm-lined drives and Spanish-style mansions, is worth a visit. Do stop in at the Royal Palm shopping center (the "Pink Plaza"), which was built to rival Palm Beach's Worth Avenue, and at the Center for the Arts. At the Royal Palm Polo Grounds, the Sunday matches in winter attract players from California, South America, England, and Australia. At halftime the spectators rush out to help stomp the grass back in place on the playing field. A champagne cart makes the rounds.

Observations: Expect to find a wide-ranging clientele at this bustling, activity-minded resort. Generally, the Cloister section of the hotel attracts an older crowd and a few honeymooners, who find it romantic. The Tower and the Beach Club, notably the latter, attract young, athletic vacationers. The Beach Club is also popular with families and conference groups. Virtually anywhere at The Boca, one will find a friendly, highly efficient staff and elegant, thoughtfully prepared cuisine.

A pool at the Beach Club (*above*) and *Mizner's Dream*, the hotel's shuttle boat (*right*).

5 *The Breakers*

Palm Beach, Florida

Know'st thou the land where the lemon trees bloom
Where the gold orange glows in the deep thicket's gloom.
Where a breeze ever soft from the blue heaven blows and the
groves are of laurel and myrtle and rose.

Johann Wolfgang von Goethe (1749 – 1832)

When the famed German poet and dramatist wrote this ode to the land that would become Palm Beach, southern Florida was a tropical swamp. Were Goethe to visit today, he would still find blue skies, lemon trees, and roses galore — the majority long stemmed in cut-glass vases. He would also discover that his unruly paradise had been primped, plucked, and manicured into Baskin-Robbins-hued perfection. The local saying goes that Mother Nature would have built Palm Beach if she had enough money.

The 5.81-square-mile island is an enclave of luxury for multidigit millionaires, and for those who like to press their noses up against one of life's most dazzling window displays. To keep out of the riffraff, the residents have talked about building toll roads, issuing identification cards, even banning automobiles. But so far, the only barricades are social, and the chauffeured Rolls-Royce Corniches and Silver Shadows still ferry the gentry of Palm Beach between their pastel mansions and the shops of Worth Avenue. "You know, I came here expecting to die," Singer Sewing Machine heir Paris Singer told his friend, architect Addison Mizner. "But I'll be damed if I feel like it."

It was Singer and Mizner together who established the character of Worth Avenue, the fabled shopping boulevard that is the heart of commercial Palm Beach. The two quixotic dreamers, inspired by the romantic architecture of the French Riviera, built stores and apartment houses in a style that blended Romanesque, Moorish, and Spanish colonial. Meandering walkways (called *vias* in these parts) lead to patios shaded by giant fantail palms. Shoppers walk beneath balconies baroque with wrought-iron grillwork; they sniff the bougainvillea-scented air and remark that, yes, it's a nice day. There is a timelessness about all this that almost defies the continually rising prices at shops like Gucci, Hermès, Cartier, and Pratesi. Yet shoppers with names like Rockefeller, Ken-

A view of the lobby (*below*) and the hotel's founder, Henry Morrison Flagler (*left*).

35

nedy, and Guest seem to take the prices in stride, regarding them as part of the whole golden fabric that is Palm Beach.

Over at The Breakers, the same attitude prevails. This buff-colored edifice, with its twin belvedere towers and loggias sweeping toward a powder-puff beach, is a metaphor for Palm Beach itself. Like Venice's aristocratic Gritti Palace or Jerusalem's war-torn King David, it is one of those hotels that is as much a symbol as it is a place to sleep. Kings and princes, duchesses and diplomats, socialites and those aspiring to the rank have strolled its columned walkways and sipped jasmine tea on its patios. Over the years, the blood at The Breakers has run as blue as the heated depths of its saltwater pool. Even today, with a Sony Walkman sighted in the lobby and occasional polyester amidst the silk, The Breakers is an institution to be reckoned with.

As one pulls up to the Palace by the Sea (the locals' name for it), a properly royal vista beckons. In an octagonal pool, a marble quartet of frolicking water nymphs holds up the bowl of a Florentine fountain. Each is supposed to symbolize a different season, though only God knows why. (In Palm Beach they'll tell you, "Summer spends the winter.") Not far from the fountain, a chauffeur waits in a convertible Bentley while another flicks some dust off the hood of a 1955 Rolls-Royce.

The hotel itself, sitting squarely on 140 immaculately landscaped acres, was designed with an Italian villa in mind, and even a doge might feel right at home. Stepping into the lobby via the porte cochere, one is suddenly in the world of Michelangelo and Donizetti. Over there, beneath the vaulted, carved ceiling, a bejeweled noblewoman adjusts her black feather boa. Phyllis Diller in purple pants and a long white mink sweeps by a fifteenth-century Flemish tapestry on her way to the elevators. An octogenarian gentleman in a blue seersucker suit, white socks and white shoes cruises the marble floors, stopping to peer out at the patio through one of the 11 door-size glass windows. A pretty woman with a Nancy Reagan hairdo and a printed chiffon dress sits at a mahogany writing table.

That evening, the rustle of silk and snapping of bow ties in the guest rooms signal the dinner hour. Those gentlemen who opt *not* to wear black tie (by no means required, but fairly common at the height of the winter season) sally forth in dark suits, perhaps tailored for them in London a few weeks earlier. Their wives, trimmed in diamonds and emeralds, favor low-cut silks and taffetas. The more fashion-conscious wear their favorite Oscar de la Renta, Mollie Parnis, or Mary McFadden picked up at the latest showing. McFadden herself once commented about the Palm Beach scene: "I think of it as a gold and diamonds city. It's the top rung of my market."

The gold and diamonds are more than adequately displayed against the backdrop of The Breakers' dining rooms. In the cavernous Main Dining Room, which easily seats 1,200, freestanding limestone columns rise toward the hand-painted beamed ceiling. In the adjacent Circle Dining Room, a vast Venetian chandelier of bronze and crystal hangs from a circular skylight and casts a pale glow on the pink tablecloths and deeper pink napkins. Through the great arched stone doorways, a parade of arriving diners is ushered past the columns to the appropriate tables. The tuxedoed captain knows without being told which pedigreed regular likes to sit here, which there. Naturally, looking around at all this well-groomed and well-orchestrated splendor, one can understand why Dustin Hoffman was refused entrance a few years ago for not having a jacket (let alone a tie).

Though Hoffman was turned away, celebrities as numerous as the rosebuds on the expanse of dining tables have sampled the chef's special lobster thermidor and soufflé glacè crème de menthe. Despite its reputation for pomp and tradition, the hotel manages to attract and amuse a wide spectrum of the world's monied rovers. Raquel Welch came for the JFK Memorial Ball — and wound up staying eight days. (She ordered bread crumbs from room service to feed to the pigeons at the beach.) Cheryl Tiegs spent many hours on the hotel's croquet court. Baseball's king, Joe DiMaggio, had a good time at The Breakers, and Jordan's monarch, King Hussein, relishes the cuisine. When Ronald Reagan showed up for a 1979 fund raiser, a Cuban bellboy had the audacity to ask for his autograph. "Find out if he can vote first!" cracked Reagan, then a presidential candidate.

This hangout for presidents, potentates, and the just-plain-rich was constructed, perhaps appropriately, by one of America's great entrepreneurs. Henry

The Circle Dining Room (*left*) and a section of the lobby (*below*).

Morrison Flagler, a New York minister's son, had made millions fairly early in life as a partner in the Standard Oil Company. In his later years, he began migrating south to Florida to escape the cold. When Flagler first visited Florida in the 1870s, he found a sleepy marshland traversed by a few rail lines with maddeningly unpredictable schedules. As he surveyed the Florida landscape, he began to envision a great mecca of tourist hotels serviced by well-run railroads. First, he focused his attention on St. Augustine, then a torpid little Spanish town. To the amazement of his friends up north, he built a grand Spanish-style inn in St. Augustine. He named it after another adventurer who had been fascinated by Florida, Ponce de Leon.

His appetite whetted, Flagler proceeded south toward Palm Beach. The railroad network he had established, the Florida East Coast Railway, reached Palm Beach in 1894. The inevitable hotel building was soon under way. The first Flagler resort to open in Palm Beach was the banana yellow Royal Poinciana. Next came a smaller hotel a short distance east of the Royal Poinciana. Called the Palm Beach Inn, its name was soon changed to The Breakers.

For the next four decades, The Breakers and its neighbor competed vigorously for the Palm Beach carriage trade, which arrived, naturally, by Flagler's railroad. In 1934 a hurricane wiped out the Poinciana. The Breakers survived. It had, by this time, withstood a number of disasters, including fires in 1903 and 1925. It was after the 1925 fire that Flagler's heirs (who own the hotel today) decided to hire a rather flamboyant New York architect named Leonard Schultze to do the rebuilding. With visions of Renaissance palazzi in his head, Schultze built a $6 million testimonial to Palm Beach's unerring faith that living well is the best revenge against fire and any other troublesome element.

Over the years, Breakers guests have assertively devoted themselves to the good life. Today, the traditions continue, especially in winter, when the hotel exhibits its most social self. In its lavish ballrooms, charity galas and luncheons follow one another like scenes in a richly costumed drama. In its dining rooms, the Sam Kart Orchestra plays "Mack the Knife" and "Yellow Bird" while ladies who believe that you cannot be too rich or too thin nibble cautiously at the calories on the gold and white china. Over by the Alcazar Lounge, the hotel's chief nightspot, stone lions guard the entrance to a pub fit for a pasha. Beneath the tentlike expanse of rainbow-hued fabric suspended from the ceiling, a brunette with a thick French accent discusses her latest divorce. Whitey, the bartender, impassively mixes her a very dry martini. "The Breakers," Whitey will say if asked how he likes his work, "is where bartenders go before they die and go to heaven."

Not everyone, of course, is so exuberant. A few of the old-timers bemoan the hotel's decision to open its doors to conference guests. They also shake their heads at the golf carts whizzing by and at the skimpy tennis outfits spotted in the lobby. The news that a European woman has been sighted topless on a distant stretch of Breakers beach delights some, and horrifies others. All in all, however, this slight unraveling of social fabric is accepted with equanimity. As Addison Mizner himself once put it: "In Florida, everything troublesome becomes trivial."

38

The Breakers

1 South County Road
Palm Beach, Florida   33480

Telephone
305-655-6611

On the Premises: Lavish as a Renaissance palace, The Breakers has 567 rooms and 41 suites. Besides the visual splendor of the surroundings, the hotel offers its guests two 18-hole golf courses, nine clay tennis courts and five all-weather ones, fishing, waterskiing, sailing, swimming at the beach or saltwater pool, and highly social rounds of croquet. In case muscles are sore at the end of the day, Bertha and Matti Pentilla, the hotel's longtime masseuse and masseur, stand by.

Rooms: Nothing could match the sheer opulence of The Breakers' lobby, dining rooms, and various ballrooms. In contrast, the guest rooms are almost subdued. Yet they are comfortable, decorated in pickled oak, pine country-French furniture, and pretty muted prints.

All the rooms are equipped with air conditioning, color television, direct-dial phones, and enormous closets. The best views are generally in the newest wing, which fronts on the water. Should you want a suite, ask for one of the four presidential ones, which are nicely appointed with brocade upholstery and Venetian prints and paintings. The water views are splendid.

Meals: The day begins at The Breakers with a large breakfast buffet (an a la carte menu is also available). A light lunch of hamburgers, sandwiches, and salads is served under umbrellas outside the seaside beach club; inside the club, a daily buffet table is spread with ham, chicken, and beef entrees, salads, and the chef's concoctions of the moment. The multicourse evening meal is beautifully presented on the hotel's gold and white china. The chef's specialties (lobster thermidor, beef Wellington, and red snapper en papillote) appear on the menu, along with entrees such as

39

Peking duck and Florida pompano. The pastry chef's vacherin glacé and Linzer torte are excellent, but the favorite seems to be the Key lime pie.

Getting There: The Breakers is a 15-minute drive from Palm Beach International Airport in West Palm Beach. Take Southern Boulevard east to Route 1A; then turn left onto Route A1A and follow it to the end; bear left onto Barton Road, then right onto County Road to The Breakers.

Money Matters: The Breakers operates on the modified American plan for most of the year. At the height of the tourist season (mid-December to early April), the cost of a double room ranges from $165 to $245. In the late spring and fall, prices drop (a double ranges from about $130 to $220); in the slower summer season, the European plan is in effect, and rates are about half the winter prices, minus meals. The hotel accepts MasterCard, Visa, and American Express.

Side Trips: Most guests head directly for the 200 shops on Worth Avenue and the 48 more in the Esplanade Arcade on the east end of Worth. After considering the Italian lace peignoirs, Oriental ivory carvings, yachts and Rolls-Royces made of chocolate, one might want to view the collection at the Henry Morrison Flagler Museum. This three-story museum, built in 1901 by the oil and railroad baron, is a must for understanding the area's history and culture. Sports fans might enjoy the Sunday matches at the Palm Beach Polo and Country Club in Wellington, about 15 miles west of town. (Palm Beach County now calls itself the Polo Capital of the Free World.)

Observations: When the winter season is in full swing, The Breakers is a highly social and glamorous place where women show off their clothes and jewels, and men their women. In 1971 The Breakers established a policy of staying open the entire year, a decision that inevitably meant accepting convention business to keep the hotel as full as possible. Generally, the conventions are booked in the slower seasons. Those who want to experience The Breakers at its most elegant should come in the peak social season. At any time, however, expect to be pampered; the hotel maintains a tradition of one employee for every guest.

The croquet court.

The Breakers

6 *The Cloister*

Sea Island, Georgia

A patch of cotton still remains on the manicured golf course. In a glass case at the clubhouse is an ivory bust of a slave girl, Nora August, carved by a Union soldier. The Clubhouse it-self was once an old corn and fodder barn constituted of tabby, a seventeenth- and eighteenth-century cement made from lime, sand, and oyster shells. By the parking lot are the ruins of a slave hospital built by the humanitarian owners of the plantation that once stood on these grounds.

Preserving these vestiges of plantation life is as important to the management, if not to the golfers, as grooming the fairways. When the course was designed, not only the old hospital walls but also a slave burial ground just off the green were left carefully untouched. Such reverence for the past is evident throughout The Cloister, the Sea Island resort that owns the club and presides over the sultry coastal isle. Ever since The Cloister opened its doors in 1928, it has maintained a regard for tradition and history that, fortunately, is good-natured rather than pompous. "There's a riddle here," volunteers Ted Wright, the hotel's managing director. "How many Sea Islanders does it take to change a light bulb? The answer is three: one to screw in the new one and two to rave about how good the old one was."

Sea Island is a tiny, ribbon-shaped spit of land 5 miles long and less than a half-mile wide. It is privately owned by the Sea Island Company, a family-run business. Besides the hotel, the only property on the island is a thriving vacation colony of 300 private homes inhabited by the likes of Bert Lance, Griffin Bell, and giants of Wall Street and industry. These cottages, as they are called, are well sheltered behind clumps of oaks and magnolias and towering palmettos. Many are made of a modern-day version of the old oyster-shell cement, known to local wisecrackers as "shabby tabby."

Secluded on the southern end of the island, the hotel is an insular and indeed cloistered environment. From the moment a guest drives across the causeway from nearby St. Simons Island, which is linked, in turn, to the Georgia main-land, he enters a world of semitropical timelessness. Through the ancient oak trees, the visitor sees the outline of a cream-colored stucco mansion with circu-lar turret and red-tiled Mediterranean roof. The afternoon sunlight plays on the Gothic windows made of leaded glass. This graceful villa, which houses the lobby, public rooms, and some guest rooms, was designed in the 1920s by the eccentric, 300-pound Florida developer, Addison Mizner. Not far away, dunes matted with vines and sandspurs flatten into a powdery beach that stretches along one side of the island. The waves of the Atlantic meander onto the sand or crash against the breakwater, depending on the tides and the elements.

This capricious sea was once an inspiration to the playwright Eugene O'Neill, who lived on Sea Island with his wife, actress Carlotta Monterey, from 1931 to 1936. In Casa Genotta, their 22-room brick cottage overlooking the ocean, O'Neill finished *Days Without End* and wrote his only comedy, *Ah Wilderness*. He worked for 24 hours at a stretch, standing at a high captain's desk. In the evenings he would unwind in the company of invited guests like Somerset Maugham, Sherwood Anderson, Lillian Gish, and Bennett Cerf. Often they would slip over to The Cloister a few streets away for an elegant dinner and a nightcap.

Over the years, The Cloister has also welcomed Presidents Coolidge, Hoover, Eisenhower, Carter, and Ford. In 1928 President Coolidge planted a Constitution Oak of the same species that furnished timbers used in Old Ironsides. Today, it is commemorated with a plaque. Ogelthorpe Oak, grown from acorns from the English gardens of General James Ogelthorpe (the British officer sent to secure Georgia for the Crown), is similarly honored.

43

Playwright Eugene O'Neill and his wife, Carlotta, were Sea Islanders in the 1930s (*above*). Guests of the era take tea in the Spanish Lounge (*right*).

An avenue of oaks shades the golf course (*left*) and a Gothic window adorns the old Cloister (*below*).

44

The Cloister

The Cloister is lavishly landscaped with gardens of lilies, snapdragons, roses, and amaryllis. This colorful backdrop is rivaled only by the wardrobe of the guests. Something about this Southern isle seems to bring out a peacockish attire virtually unmatched at any other resort. The minute a gentleman arrives at The Cloister, he dons the requisite pink pants and green linen jacket, or green pants and pink linen jacket. The racier types flaunt trousers patterned with porpoises, spouting whales, garden rakes, sailboats, or crabs. Their ties are spotted with everything from sea horses and lilies to tennis rackets. The women, more subdued in basic pastel skirts, and polo shirts, shorts, appear to admire their spouses' display of plummage, and encourage shopping for more splendor in The Cloister's shops.

Sartorial daring aside, The Cloister is a place of rather sedate pursuits. In its Colonial parlor filled with Queen Anne wing chairs, Chippendale chests, and gold-leaf mirrors, there is an air of quiet reserve. Beneath the exposed beams of pecky cypress, the guests read, play canasta, work jigsaw puzzles, and genuinely seem to forget that the outside world exists. In the Spanish Lounge, they sit in the old carved chairs and sip afternoon tea. The Gothic windows, more suitable for a medieval church or monastery, lend a somberness to the room.

Over in the main dining room, the flames in the Italian stone fireplace cast a glow on the dark Mediterranean chairs. As the orchestra plays "Blue Moon," a couple who have been visiting The Cloister for decades are seated at their regular table. The pickled ginger they like is placed, as always, by their plates. "This is a time capsule," observes one longtime Cloister guest, who nevertheless bemoans the fact that black tie is "encouraged" but no longer required on Thursday and Saturday nights in the dining rooms. "Now you'll see guys in bowling shirts."

A few hours after dinner each evening, the staff puts out milk and homemade gingersnaps and graham crackers as a little bedtime snack. Stronger liquids are available, naturally, for those who want to settle down in the bar and lounge areas. Over strawberry daiquiris, planter's punch, and stingers (the drinks match the colorful clothes in these parts), guests who have been returning to The Cloister for 20 and 30 years chitchat. The conversation is genteel. "No sex," volunteers Rae Outlaw, a cocktail waitress who has been slinging stingers at the hotel for nearly 20 years. "Just golf."

If The Cloister ever approaches anything faintly resembling raucousness, it is during the summer months or spring vacation, when families descend on the hotel. The paths are filled with bicyclists, and the beaches and two swimming pools with giggling children. The management supplements the abundant sporting activities with an assortment of social activities (offered year round). The hotel arranges needlepoint classes, cooking courses, slimnastics, bridge tournaments, painting lessons, golf clinics, flower-arranging demonstrations, and dance contests. During Big Band weeks, the men put on white dinner jackets and the women swishy ankle-length chiffon dresses and rhinestone sandals, and recapture another era.

Years ago, the scene of all this circumspect gaiety was little more than marshes and goat pastures. The man who put it on the tourist map was Howard Coffin, a farm boy from the small Quaker community of West Milton, Ohio. As historian Harold Martin recounts his progress in *This Happy Isle, The Story of Sea Island and the Cloister*, Coffin was a whiz at fixing farm equipment and later grew into a talented designer of motor cars. He became the chief engineer of the Hudson Motor Company. During a trip to Chatham County, Georgia, in 1910 to watch his company's cars perform in the Vanderbilt Cup competition, his chauffeur suggested a fishing trip to one of the islands. Coffin agreed, and became forever hooked by the untamed beauty of the coastline. Before long he had purchased Sapelo Island, a mostly empty wilderness used as a hunting preserve. He soon developed his island with the help of a young cousin, Alfred W. Jones, called Bill.

Coffin and Jones gradually turned their attention to another coastal island that had been variously named Fifth Creek Island, Isle of Palms, Long Island, and Glynn Isle. In 1926 Coffin bought it and renamed it Sea Island. He figured he would build a "cottage" colony on Sea Island and a "friendly little hotel" where people could stay while picking out lots. Bill Jones was dispatched to Florida to see if the mighty architect Addison Mizner, who had just finished Boca Raton's Cloister Inn (later The Boca Raton Hotel and Club), might design Coffin's inn. He readily accepted and proceeded to design an estate suitable for a Spanish don. Mizner, after all, was the man the *Saturday Evening Post* once described as having "transformed Palm Beach from the rich man's Coney Island into a perpetual World's Fair of architecture."

Out of sentiment, perhaps, for his Florida venture, Mizner persuaded Coffin to name the hotel The Cloister. From the moment it opened in 1928, The Cloister was a success.

In the years to come, more rooms were built in guest houses and in three beach houses—Retreat, Hamilton, and Harrington—named for antebellum plantations whose lands are now encompassed by the Sea Island Company. Along came tennis courts, golf courses, and yes, television, but only in the lounges, clubrooms, and parlor suites. It was the feeling of the management that The Cloister was a place where people gathered and made friends, and that TV throughout the rooms would defeat that purpose.

Howard Coffin, who died in 1937, most likely would have approved. The Sea Island Company, under the stewardship of Bill Jones and later Jones's son, Bill, Jr., has never forgotten founder Coffin's desire for a "friendly little hotel." "People who like slot machines, bright lights, and lots of glitter shouldn't come here," cautions Bill Jones, Jr., Sea Island's president.

So far, the slot machine crowd seems to have gotten the message. A quieter clientele flocks back year after year for the Friday-night plantation suppers (shrimp mull, fried chicken, and six gospel singers crooning spirituals at a seaside picnic site), and the Tuesday-and Thursday-night bingo games (the price, $2 for six games, hasn't gone up in 10 years). They also like the sand-sculpture contests, chip 'n putt tournaments, and all-round joviality.

Many of the regulars consider the resort a second home. One day, a newcomer was rude enough to put his feet up on the mahogany butler's-tray coffee table in the Colonial Lounge. It had, after all, been a tough 18-holes of golf. No sooner had he crossed his ankles and leaned back than a woman rushed to his side. "At The Cloister," pronounced the old-timer as she scooped his feet off the furniture, "we don't *do* that."

Sea Island, Georgia   31561

Telephone
912-638-3611

On the Premises: A world removed on a lush, semitropical Georgia island, The Cloister has 264 rooms and 100 suites. It has four, nine-hole golf courses at the Sea Island Club, which is just across the bridge on St. Simons Island. There are two swimming pools and a beach that winds around the island. In addition, The Cloister offers stables with 60 horses, 18 competition tennis courts, bicycling, fishing boats, skeet and trapshooting, lawn bowling, sailing (Sunfish and catamarans), and nature walks.

Rooms: Many of the 300 exclusive, privately owned homes on the island (two to five bedrooms each) are available for rent through The Cloister. These cottages, as they are called, are ideal for families seeking secluded quarters outfitted with everything from king-size brass beds to Jacuzzis and private pools. At The Cloister itself, there is a wide range of choices in accommodations. Some guests would stay nowhere other than the main building, with its proximity to the various parlors and dining rooms and the enclosed garden patio. The rooms here tend to have old-world charm. In the newer accommodations, called beach houses and guest houses, white bamboo chairs, seashell lamps, and soft pastel floral draperies and bedspreads create a summerlike effect. Walk-in closets, spacious baths with collapsible clotheslines, twin vanities, and a personal safe in every room are special touches.

Meals: Breakfast is served both buffet style and from a menu, which offers a wide range of selections such as smoked ham, salt mackerel filets, kippered herring, buckwheat cakes, buttermilk biscuits, and homemade fruit, coconut, and peanut Danish. The full-course lunches at The Cloister start with soups, melon, or perhaps smoked fish, and move on to entrees that include Chesapeake Bay scallops Provençal, broiled breast of capon on eggplant, and roast loin of Jersey pork. The dinner menu, which changes daily, is Continental with a strong emphasis on seafood. The chef prepares local delicacies like shrimp mull (a spicy creole concoction), she-crab soup (male crabs are used, too), and oyster potpie.

Getting There: By automobile, take Interstate 95 to Brunswick, Georgia, and then the

47

The Cloister

causeway to Sea Island. The island is halfway between Savannah, Georgia, and Jacksonville, Florida. By air, a commuter line lands at McKinnon Airport, 3 miles from the hotel. The nearest commercial airport is at Jacksonville, 70 miles away. (The hotel will send a limousine on request.)

Money Matters: The Cloister operates on the full American plan (three meals a day, plus afternoon tea and bedtime snacks). The price of a double room averages about $100 per person in the busy spring and summer seasons. Credit cards are not accepted.

Side Trips: The surrounding countryside is rich with historical sites. On nearby St. Simons Island is Fort Frederica, a pre-Revolutionary British fortification that served as the base for both offensive and defensive opera-

tions against the Spanish in Florida. Farther afield is Jekyll Island, where an elite club composed of Morgans, Astors, Vanderbilts, and Rockefellers was founded in 1886 (the island today is a state park). Blackbeard Island to the north is named for the notorious pirate Edward Teach, or Blackbeard, who is said to have stashed his booty here.

Observations: The Cloister is a genteel and conservative-minded resort justifiably proud of its history and traditions. It is not the place for excessively loud partying or lots of glitter. The clientele changes somewhat with the seasons. In winter and spring, a core of regulars, including many Northern couples, return year after year. In spring and summer, families, mostly Southern, descend on The Cloister.

7 *The Homestead*

Hot Springs, Virginia

On the hazy spring morning Elizabeth Taylor visited The Homestead, her eyes matched the deep purple of the far-off Allegheny peaks, and her words were as gushing as the famous hot springs from which the area derives its name. "I consider this the Versailles of America," declared the actress, ever mindful that constituents of her then husband, Virginia Senator John Warner, were listening. When another famous guest, the late President Lyndon Baines Johnson, descended onto the sweeping lawn in his helicopter, the commotion was only slightly less pronounced. "Mah Gaawd," drawled LBJ. "What a spread. Lady Bird will sure be sorry she missed *this!*"

Over the years a parade of distinguished visitors have been similarly awed by the white-columned Georgian hotel constructed of dusty red Virginia brick. The Duke and Duchess of Windsor spent an entire month at The Homestead in 1943, strolling contentedly along its winding paths and trails. When they were ready to take their leave, a bill was proffered. "Now what do I do with *this?*" muttered His Highness, seemingly aghast. (The account remains unsettled to this day.)

America's royalty, too, has come to call. Four presidents have visited The Homestead while in office: William Howard Taft, Woodrow Wilson, Warren G. Harding, and LBJ. Franklin Roosevelt, Richard Nixon, and Gerald Ford signed the guest register, before or after they served in the White House. Ford, in fact, arrived one week before the resignation of his predecessor, Richard Nixon. He headed directly for the golf course. For former Secretary of State Henry Kissinger, The Homestead was a place to temporarily submerge the world's cares in a hot mineral tub. His equestrienne wife, Nancy, rode expertly along trails frequented largely by gray squirrels and an occasional skunk. Another horse lover, Paul Mellon, brought his own mount, Christmas Goose, and won The Homestead's 100-mile trail ride three years in a row.

Given its heritage, The Homestead is a surprisingly low-key and quiet place. The true devotees, those who return year after year to sit in the white wicker chairs on the veranda, like to call it The Home. Each afternoon at teatime, they sink into a squishy chair in the 211-foot-long chandelier-hung lobby and nibble cinnamon toast and cookies. While a string quartet plays Mozart and Strauss, they doze off by the fire or play backgammon. "It's a place to relax," says author and newspaper columnist Joseph Alsop, who has been vacationing at The Homestead for 15 years. "I send down a crate of books from Washington and I don't do a damn thing except read and take walks."

A feeling of warmth is all-pervasive. Despite the grandeur of its lobby (called the Great Hall by the staff), The Homestead is by no means formidable. The grand staircases creak just the right amount and the endless parlors and sitting rooms are outfitted with armchairs and comfy Queen Anne love seats. One can easily pluck a book from the shelf and almost, but not quite, contemplate putting one's feet up on the mahogany coffee table. Only the hum of a Dow Jones ticker hidden discreetly behind a screen near a fireplace reminds one that this is, after all, a hotel that caters to its share of conference guests.

Even the staff feels like family. Mr. Nelson, the resident manager, has been at The Homestead for 29 years. If he sees a familiar face at check-in, he is right there with a warm handshake and a question about the kids. In the dining room, 77-year-old Joseph H. (Mack) McMillan has been serving cured Virginia hams, Maryland crab, fresh Allegheny mountain trout, and the chef's special spoonbread for more than 50 years—and bringing out the silver finger bowls to wash away the crumbs. Mack remembers serving Mrs. Cornelius Vanderbilt,

The Georgian clock tower and main hotel (*above*) and the Zander Room (*above right*).

who spent many summers at The Homestead ("She was *not* a liberal tipper," he recalls), as well as John D. Rockefeller, Sr., also not know for his largess. "Once, I even lent a dollar to him!" Mack remembers with a shake of the head.

Another Homestead old-timer is white-haired Miss Lena. Her unique preserve is the hotel's celebrated spa building, constructed right over the warm mineral springs. Padding around in her bare feet, Miss Lena leads adventurous guests to porcelain tubs built in special cubicles with drains in the floor. Head tilted back, a cool cloth on the forehead, the guest sits luxuriantly while the waters gush up through a spout and empty over the sides of the tub. All those childhood taboos about not letting the water run over the tub are deliciously forgotten for 10 minutes. (A longer soak requires a doctor's permission.)

Fresh from the tub, feeling tingly, one heads for the massage table. Miss Lena reaches into a bucket of salt mixed with a little water and administers a

rub. "What's this supposed to do?" asks a Californian who thought she had seen everything. "It helps the circulation," she is told matter-of-factly. Slightly dubious, but feeling good, the woman heads for a metal shower contraption outfitted with 16 nozzles. Miss Lena regulates them and also sprays the woman with a special pressurized hose.

For the truly adventurous, The Homestead has a roomful of exercise equipment unparalleled anywhere. This is the Zander Room, named after the Swedish physician who designed the collection in the mid-nineteenth century. Gustav Zander's cast-iron machines, outfitted with solid brass fittings, hand-painted finials, and deep green mohair seats, were once widely used in Europe. During World War II, however, most spas that were equipped with them were destroyed. The Zander Room at The Homestead was constructed in 1911. Today, almost unchanged, it strikes the newcomer as a cross between the Marquis de Sade's basement and a Beverly Hills health spa. But appearances aside, it provides a good workout. An attendant stands by to demonstrate how to use the various weights, pulleys, pressure machines, and bicycles. "To my way of thinking," says a European woman who has tried spas all over the world, "nothing beats the Zander Room, because if you get tired of working out you can just rest and look around, almost as if you were in a museum."

Refreshed from the workout, a guest might then take a stroll to the hamlet of Hot Springs, just down the hill from the hotel. There is no need for a traffic

53

light in Hot Springs. In fact, they tell you in these parts that there is not one light in all of Bath County. Drivers poke along the main drag, pulling over to the curb to chat with a neighbor or a friend. Over the old train station, where the Chesapeake and Ohio used to hiss to a stop, a cluster of Homestead visitors prepare to do some serious shopping. The old depot has been given a coat of fresh creamy yellow paint and renovated into a little mall of boutiques that offer rag dolls, toys, sweaters, even calico wreaths. The old bank building, likewise, has taken a turn. It now houses Sam Snead's Tavern, a snappy, wood-paneled restaurant and bar owned jointly by the golf pro and his son, both native sons. Naturally, the tavern sells Sam Snead T-shirts, tote bags, and copies of the pro's book, *Golf Begins at Forty*.

So far, no one is selling little plastic pouches filled with water from the original hot springs. As the story goes, it was a sixteenth-century Indian brave who first discovered the healing qualities of these tepid waters. The Spring of Strength, as the Indians called the waters, gradually became a sanctuary. The taking of scalps near the springs was taboo. By the eighteenth century, white men had settled in the area and had discovered the springs.

The first hotel in the area was a rudimentary inn built in 1776. By 1832, an enterprising doctor named Thomas Goode had acquired the property and distributed pamphlets advertising the medical benefits of the sprints. Plantation owners and farmers came from all over the state seeking cures for rheumatism, gout, cholera, dropsy, hepatitis, dyspepsia, and arthritis. Their wives sought help for various vaguely described "female ailments."

As word of the waters spread, a carefully proscribed social ritual developed. Ladies and gentlemen would travel a circuit from the hot springs to various other mineral pools in the surrounding valleys. At the so-called warm springs, about 5 miles from the hot springs, Thomas Jefferson is said to have been the designer of the octagonal gentlemen's pool house constructed in 1732. (The women's bath, with its separate gazebo, wasn't built until 1832.) In these small frame bathhouses, the bathers paddled about or hung from ropes strung across the waters. Attendant waiters floated out mint juleps on cork trays. An especially picturesque description of this social scene was described by a writer of the period, who used the nom de plume Peregrine Prolix:

"The water is five feet deep for the gentlemen, four for the ladies. The two sexes bathe alternately, spaces of two hours each being allotted, from 6 A.M. to 10 P.M. You may take three baths a day without injury. To bathe comfortably, you should have a large cotton morning gown, a cashmere shawl pattern lined with crimson, a fancy Greek cap, Turkish slippers, and a pair of loose pantaloons; a garb that will not consume much time in doffing. . ."

The pleasures and peccadilloes of the baths were rivaled by the entertainment at The Homestead. The old frame inn had gradually given way to a larger wood hotel, and then to the red-brick structure with its various wings and clock tower that stands today. By the early twentieth century, The Homestead had become one of America's grand-scale resorts. The visiting gentry were chauffeured about in carriages and buckboards. In the evenings, they danced the cotillion in the grand ballroom. When it was time for liquid refreshments, a gentleman might signal for his own personal bottle to be brought out from its cabinet. (The local laws did not allow the serving of infusions in public places until much later.)

Southern gentlemen being no different from any other, there was a certain hankering for gambling now and then. Money is said to have passed hands on occasion in the old casino building. About twice a year, a much-anticipated event known as the Tray Race allowed a fair traffic in Calcutta pools. At Tray-Race time, the staff of black waiters would balance 30- to 60-pound trays of cutlery and fruit and run 60 yards in five measured heats. Gradually, however, both waiters and some guests objected to this custom, and the races were abandoned.

Today, the vestiges of competition take place on the tennis courts, the golf links, or the riding trails. In winter the scene shifts to Warm Springs Mountain, where The Homestead pioneered Southern skiing in 1959 with a 3,200-foot slope and snow guns. There are now four runs of varying difficulty and a double chair lift. Instructors stand by, as they do at the large skating rink at the foot of the beginner's slope. There, they gently coach the children and encourage rusty adults who last wobbled on ice as children at their grandmother's pond. Sometimes, grandma herself is waiting in the glassed-in chalet. Sipping cider and munching doughnuts, she is in bliss.

Of all the poignant moments at The Homestead, one weary traveler will never forget the time she arrived as the hands of the grandfather clock approached midnight. A sudden storm, a delayed plane, a long drive from the airport, and the evening had slipped away. Inside the Great Hall, the fireplaces still crackled, though the last guest had gone to bed. In the lounge area, four tuxedoed gentlemen, members of the hotel's string quartet, talked quietly in a corner. But for the musicians, this room, too, was empty. Suddenly, they saw the lone traveler, weary from her journey and desiring a bedtime brandy, sinking down into a chair. As if they had never stopped, they stood, picked up the last note of "Green Sleeves," and played on. It might have been a scene out of *Last Year at Marienbad*, reshot in the Alleghenies.

Hot Springs, Virginia   24445

Telephone

703-839-5500

The Homestead

On the Premises: Imposing in its architecture, homey in ambience, The Homestead offers its guests 546 rooms, including 77 suites. The resort has three 18-hole golf courses, 19 tennis courts (all outdoor), two outdoor pools and one indoor one, eight tenpin bowling alleys, an Olympic-size skating rink, skeet and trap shooting, fishing in a 3-mile stream stocked with rainbow trout, hiking, carriage rides, horseback riding, even Southern skiing.

Rooms: The rooms at The Homestead are comfortable but by no means slick. (Only in the new conference wing is there a veneer of modernity.) Mostly, the accommodations are cozy with flowered wallpaper and big old bureaus. The most coveted rooms are the ones with the sunny parlors and the screened porches overlooking the mountains. If you want a suite, ask for 901, a two-bedroom sprawl where Mrs. Cornelius Vanderbilt stayed for many summers.

Meals: Virginia cured bacon, of course, is on the breakfast menu, along with buckwheat cakes, grits, steamed finnan haddie, grilled fresh striped bass, and just about anything else you might want. The lunch and dinner menus change daily and are multicourse and Continental. The chef occasionally prepares Southern specialties, such as Allegheny trout, Maryland crab claws, and double breast of chicken with glazed bananas and corn fritters. The cornbread, sourdough bread, and crusty French loaves are all baked in The Homestead's ovens, as is the melba toast.

Getting There: The Homestead is a five-hour drive from Washington, D.C., and is on U.S. 220 north. By air, the resort is serviced by Greenbrier Airport in Lewisburg, West Virginia, about an hour away, and by nearby Ingalls Field, where small corporate planes can land. (There is also a commuter air service from Washington to Ingalls.)

Money Matters: The price of a room at The Homestead includes three full meals a day and afternoon tea. A standard double ranges from $96 to $123 per person, per day. Credit cards are not accepted.

Side Trips: Lexington, Virginia, a carefully restored historic small town about an hour away, is the site of the Virginia Military Institute and Washington and Lee University. In Warm Springs, about 5 miles down the road from The Homestead, there are two famous bathing pools open to the public in summer. Another dalliance is a long ride through countryside dotted with cabins and farmhouses and an occasional antique shop selling mountain glass and oak furniture.

Observations: This is a grand, historic resort that places great stock in its past. Its public rooms are proper, even a little prim. With its extraordinary recreational facilities, The Homestead is a great place for families, especially at Christmastime when the Great Hall, as the lobby is called, is festooned with an enormous Christmas tree and aflutter with rounds of eggnog and caroling. Remember that The Homestead, though lively, is not a glittery place.

8 *The Greenbrier*

White Sulphur Springs, West Virginia

They came 300 strong, in limousines and in 14 private railroad cars. Pedigreed, pampered, and trailed by maids and valets, the titans of Washington and Wall Street, Hollywood and high society, swept up the grand staircase of The Greenbrier hotel. In the course of that memorable four-day April weekend in 1948, the Duke of Windsor, an amateur hand at the drums, played a credible rendition of "How Are Things in Glocca Morrah?" at a diamond ball. Industrial giants Angier Biddle Duke and Nicky du Pont talked shop near a portrait of an eighteenth-century gentleman, attributed to Gilbert Stuart. Bing Crosby, dressed in an old red crewneck and brown cardigan, was heckled on the golf course by a tiny dog, which barked ferociously at his shots. He later confided, according to the prominent social historian Cleveland Amory, that he had been awed by the weekend. "I had to wash and iron my shirt," Crosby confessed, "*before* sending it to the laundry." The Old Groaner was also intimidated by his maid. "She used a lorgnette," he reported, "to look under the bed."

The occasion for this lavish house party was the postwar reopening of The Greenbrier. The privileged guests invited to the gala at the historic old hotel, which dates back to before the Civil War, were in the mood to celebrate. The ladies and gentlemen proved themselves an especially jovial bunch. "Ex-wives of ex-husbands, and ex-husbands of ex-wives," said Mrs. William Randolph Hearst, Jr., the former Mrs. Igor Cassini, "rubbed elbows like olives in the same bottle." Her ex-spouse, Hearst society reporter Igor Cassini, was also impressed. Writing under his pen name, Cholly Knickerbocker, he proclaimed: "We doubt that the Sultan of Turkey, the Emperor of China, or the Czar of Russia, when those fabulous courts were at their peaks, ever attempted anything on a more colossal scale."

Overstated perhaps, but forgivable. The Greenbrier is the kind of spread that inspires loftiness. The flags of the original 13 colonies flutter in front of its columned portico. The hotel itself, a sweep of white Georgian architecture, sits like a small European palace atop a rolling hillside. The sculpted beds of tulips, hyacinths, or amaryllis (depending on the season) in the center of the circular driveway are a still life against the white. By the front door, the sand in the two antique porcelain ashtrays is imprinted with a delicately curved G, the Greenbrier logo. A porter replaces the sand and the G at the least sign of use.

Inside its parlors and ballrooms, the heels of kings, princes, and sheiks have clicked across the marble floors. Modern-day statesmen such as former Secretary of State Alexander Haig have migrated over from Pennsylvania Avenue to

In August 1908, President William Howard Taft (*seated in armchair*) visited with (*left to right*) Major General Clarence R. Edwards, Mrs. Taft, West Virginia Congressman Joseph Holt Gaines, and Mrs. Gaines at the "Old White."

Bob Hope, unidentified couple, and the Duchess and Duke of Windsor were among the guests at a Greenbrier party in 1953; Meyer Davis, the society bandleader, is on the far right.

relieve the pressures of government. (He played tennis and nibbled white grapes especially flown in from Washington, D.C.) When the U.S. State Department wanted a luxurious place to gather the Iranian hostages for a 90-day follow-up, they selected The Greenbrier. The government perhaps figured that besides the ample golf and tennis facilities, and enough walking and jogging trails to fill a full-color map (available at the front desk), The Greenbrier offered a south-of-the-Mason-Dixon line pace. Each evening around dinner hour, discreet signs appear in the hallways reading: "Shhh . . . it's sleepytime down South."

"It's antebellum. It has a majestic quality," notes Carleton Varney, the New York decorator who has been responsible for The Greenbrier's interior design since the 1960s. The visitor might well concur. Entering the upper lobby, one can, if the hour is right, hear the strains of a string quartet and see waitresses in starched aprons dispensing tea. The guests balance cups against a backdrop of aquamarine walls and white columns. They gaze in the direction of a Sèvres jardiniere on a mantelpiece, or at an oil of George Washington painted by Gilbert Stuart's daughter, Jane. They circle around the Cantonese bowl on the central mahogany table, and fan out into lemon- and lime-hued salons. Just off the lobby in the Victorian writing room, a graying gentleman in blue blazer, white flannel slacks, and highly polished black tassel loafers leans against the marble fireplace beneath an ormolu French chandelier. His wife, spying the insouciance, rushes over to brush off his arm. A few salons away in the presidents' parlor, a trio of women wearing pastel linen skirts and blue linen blazers peruse the room as if it were a museum. They pause in front of the seventeenth-century coromandel screen, the Queen Anne Chippendale table, and the Baccarat clock over the fireplace.

Downstairs in the lower lobby, a different mood prevails. This is where guests check in and out, and also browse through the row of boutiques; they wind up, possibly, at the ice-cream parlor and coffee shop at the far end. The decor in the lobby is a splash of whimsy. Benches upholstered in green and white fabric like the awnings of a Cape Cod summerhouse are scattered here and there. Pheasants are patterned on durable red and green vinylized sofas. Bellboys scurry around with luggage. A contingent of about a dozen joggers, members of a conference group in residence at the hotel, bend and stretch a bit before sprinting down the steps and along the driveway. Women in short tennis skirts and men in madras golf pants hurry to meet their partners. A small boy in a Snoopy sweat shirt is crying inconsolably. It appears that the chocolate Easter egg the size of a grown-up that he saw on his last visit is no longer in the upstairs lobby. His father explains, as patiently as possible, that Easter is over.

Should the boy return at Halloween, he will find 50-pound pumpkins. At Christmas, a 27-foot tree, wassail bowls, garlands of holly, and literally hundreds of poinsettias (grown in the hotel's three greenhouses) will be on display. He might also find an ice sculpture on the lawn.

Adults, too, appreciate the festiveness, part of The Greenbrier's year-round eagerness to give its guests a good time. Despite the historic backdrop, this is no place for musty antiquarians. The hotel operates a little like a cruise ship, offering scheduled happy hours, mountaintop hoedowns, wine tastings, lectures on antiques, even cooking courses taught by Julie Dannenbaum, a well-known Philadelphia chef. The Greenbrier's sporting life encompasses everything from bowling to carriage rides through a countryside lush with lilacs, crab apples and weeping cherry trees. Any muscles found ailing at the end of an active day can be soothed at the Greenbrier Spa, a spotless, clinic-like wing containing dressing rooms and cubicles for massage tables and mineral baths. The spa even offers a special package for those who indulged too late and too much the night before in the Old White Club, The Greenbrier's stately, chandelier-hung nightclub. "Ask for the 'Morning After Preservation,'" reads the brochure. This includes a steam bath, sauna, and "Old White Club Massage."

Before it's time to hit the Old White again, guests congregate for dinner in a columned Georgian salon the color of a perfectly ripened peach. Here, the old and new South meet with a cheerful acknowledgment that the Civil War is long over. In one corner, three generations of black women talk quietly over cognac

The Presidents' Parlor.

and praline cake. Their waitress, a white woman, is more concerned with serving the hotel's requisite after-dinner finger bowls than with the irony that a century ago this never would have happened. In another corner, an elderly Southern gentleman whose grandfather surely presided over a plantation, dines alone on chicken sautéed in bourbon. In the center of the room, eight neurosurgeons attending a medical conference at The Greenbrier prove, a little loudly, that shop can be talked anywhere. Later it's time, perhaps, for a mint julep.

Years ago, the strongest liquid consumed on the grounds was a tepid water that smelled, and tasted, like rotten eggs. This sulphur spring that eventually gave the town its name was first discovered by a tribe of Indians following a buffalo trail. In 1778 a white woman, Amanda Anderson, wife of a British sea captain, decided to visit the spring in the hopes that its reported rejuvenative qualities would cure her rheumatism. As the legend goes, the waters did the job. Before long, a cluster of resort cottages grew up around the spring to house the pilgrims seeking similar cures. (These cottages still stand today and have been modernized and turned into Greenbrier guest quarters.) The first real hotel at White Sulphur Springs was a frame mansion, 400 feet long, known as the Old White. General Robert E. Lee frequented it in the post–Civil War era, as did a bevy of Southern belles seeking husbands.

By the twentieth century, the Old White was in the hands of the Chesapeake & Ohio Railway, which decided to expand and build an adjacent hotel. (The resulting 250-room structure is the center wing of the present Greenbrier.) Then, in 1922, the Old White was unable to pass a fire test and was torn down — an event that left many wet eyes in the South. Two decades later, the

C & O sold The Greenbrier to the U.S. government to use as an Army hospital, then repurchased it in 1946.

Time and the Army had taken their toll, and a massive redecorating of the hotel was soon under way. The woman given $11 million dollars and more or less free reign to do the job right was Dorothy Draper, a socialite from Tuxedo Park who had become one of New York's top decorators. Mrs. Draper had a vivid imagination, not to mention enough zest to rankle staid Chesapeake & Ohio officials. What, they wondered, were all those pinks doing with reds? What were all those blues doing beside kelly greens? Undaunted, Mrs. Draper announced that her theme for The Greenbrier would be "romance and rhododendrons." She blithely proceeded to design a wall covering patterned with the West Virginia state flower, and splashed it all over the hallways.

Today, the rhododendrons flourish, along with other Draper signatures like pineapples (ornamenting gold chandeliers and mirrors) and swaths of carpeting and fabrics the colors of summer fruit. Her talented young assistant, Carleton Varney, who took over Dorothy Draper's firm after her death in 1968, continues in the same mode. On the theory that "pink has never threatened a man's masculinity," he has used it liberally in the guest rooms, no two of which are alike. Varney also favors capricious, brightly colored wallpapers with names like Nancy's Fancy, Tulip Time Blue, and Geranium Quilt.

Stately yet not stuffy, The Greenbrier has long appealed to those who like a little sparkle with their decorum. President Eisenhower, Ella Fitzgerald, Prince Rainier and the late Princess Grace, Joan Crawford (who demanded, and got, four down pillows) have all found it a place to unwind.

Vice-President Hubert Humphrey also let his hair down at The Greenbrier. After snacking on bowls of his beloved popcorn (thoughtfully placed in his suite by the management), the veep announced his hankering to go turkey shooting. Because Humphrey was not known as a marksman, eyebrows were raised, but mouths remained shut. The vice-president and a guide headed off to the woods. As the afternoon waned and the hunter repeatedly missed his mark, a plan swung into action. The staff rustled up a rather geriatric turkey, untied its legs, and sent it trotting directly in front of Humphrey. He missed. The turkey was rounded up and unleashed again. Humphrey missed. Finally, on the third try, he got his mark and returned euphoric to the hotel. At The Greenbrier, the story is cited as an example that hotelkeeping is a fine and highly delicate art in White Sulphur Springs.

White Sulphur Springs,
West Virginia   24986

Telephone
304-536-1110

On the Premises: This historic Southern hotel has 700 rooms, 61 suites, and 52 cottages. Its recreational facilities are extensive. The Greenbrier has two swimming pools, three 18-hole championship golf courses, 20 tennis courts (including 5 indoor ones), as well as horseback riding, skeet and trapshooting, indoor bowling, fishing in streams or a lake, ice-skating, cross-country skiing, hiking, and sleigh and carriage rides through the rural West Virginia countryside. The hotel's mineral-bath department has saunas, massages, and soaks in tubs filled with the sulphur-rich waters from which the area gets its name. Guests interested in The Greenbrier's heritage can meet with the hotel's resi-

dent historian, Dr. Robert Conte, who also organizes tours and slide presentations.

Rooms: Fancifully decorated by Carleton Varney, the accommodations are both quaint and comfortable. Many have four-poster beds, antique English tables, and a mélange of American, Chinese, and French art objects. If you *must* sleep where the Monaco royal family did, ask for the four-bedroom State Suite, furnished with Queen Anne love seats, silk wing chairs, and antique Canton ginger jars. Or, opt for Valley View, actually a private estate that comes with its own Cadillac Seville for use during one's stay. Valley View has a living room, a dining room that can ac-

63

commodate 24, a porch and terrace (replete with fountain), four master bedrooms, a kitchen, and an executive boardroom.

Meals: The Allegheny brook trout you fished for so eagerly also appears on the breakfast menu, along with selections such as corned-beef hash, waffles, and many varieties of eggs. Waitresses dispense homemade pumpkin muffins, Danish, and honey buns from piping-hot roll warmers. At lunchtime, sandwiches and salads are available in the coffee shop or at the golf club. (During the winter season, the main dining room is open on certain days for lunch.) The six-course dinners are Continental with a Southern touch: leg of lamb with plantation spoon-

bread appears on the menu, as does Maryland crab served over Virginia ham. The cornbread and beaten biscuits are, presumably, just like Mammy made.

Getting There: The Greenbrier is on Route 60, 1 mile from Interstate 64. By air, the hotel is serviced by the Greenbrier Valley Airport in Lewisburg, 12 miles away. There are daily nonstop Piedmont jets to Lewisburg from New York, Atlanta, and Washington, D.C.

Money Matters: Breakfast and dinner, along with daily tea, are included in the price of a room at The Greenbrier. A standard double ranges from $94 to $123 per person, per day. The hotel accept MasterCard, Visa, and American Express.

Side Trips: On The Greenbrier grounds, but somehow a world removed, is the Creative Arts Colony, a picturesque group of cottages dating back to 1813. A weaver, brass worker, potter, painter, and designer of dollhouses and miniatures all work on the premises. Farther afield is Charlottesville, Virginia, home of the University of Virginia and Monticello, Thomas Jefferson's home.

Observations: The Greenbrier is a lively and bustling place with a sophisticated veneer. It is by no means the vacation spot for someone who seeks a highly informal, down-home atmosphere. Because of its size, The Greenbrier does a thriving conference business, meaning that there may be small lines at times at the checkout counter and restaurant. Yet the efficient staff is adept at handling large groups, and quickly makes everyone feel welcome and at home.

9

The Arizona Biltmore

Phoenix, Arizona

I t was 1929, not a propitious year for new businesses, when the Packards and Pierce Arrows first pulled up to the front door. The elegant ladies and gentlemen attending the

opening-night party came with a Gatsbyesque edge of gaiety, blissfully unaware of the stock market crash just around the corner. The desert breezes were soothingly warm that night and life, temporarily, was as it should be. On the menu was lobster thermidor, boned squab, and creamed artichokes. Appropriate liquids were served—even though Prohibition was still the law of the land. While the guests imbibed, Chief Joe Seckuku and his band of Hopi Indians entertained. So did a South American tenor named Señor Pedraza and a group called Garcia's Spanish Strollers. At one point in the festivities, a trimotor Ford airplane circled the hotel several times and dropped a huge golden key. On cue, a Hopi Indian runner scaled the Biltmore walls, recovered the key, and presented it to the manager.

Even more curious than the festivities was the hotel itself. The partygoers found themselves viewing a starkly angular structure built of textured concrete blocks. Inside, the same gray chunks, immediately nicknamed Biltmore blocks, formed beamed ceilings, columns, and balconies. In the lobby and dining room, the ceilings sparkled with gold leaf.

This dramatic design, which guests called everything from Aztec to art deco, was the fulfillment of a dream. Two brothers, Charles and Warren McArthur, whose father once held the Dodge franchise in Arizona, envisioned a luxury hotel in the north Phoenix foothills. At the time, Phoenix was just a small commercial center for the nearby copper, cotton, and cattle industries, hardly the setting for a grand-scale resort. But the brothers persisted. They called upon a third sibling, Albert Chase McArthur, who had studied with Frank Lloyd Wright in his Oak Park, Illinois, studio. As the work progressed, the McArthurs asked Wright himself to consult. "The work on the project consumed all of his time," Olgivanna Lloyd Wright, the architect's widow, has written. "Naturally, he discussed with me some of the problems confronting him relating to his position behind the scenes, with Albert Chase McArthur as the architect in charge. It was a very difficult task for him since my husband, as we all know, was never famous as a man who willingly made any compromises."

The finished product was a triumph not only of diplomacy but also of design. However, shortly after the hotel opened, the McArthurs and their financial backers, the Biltmore Hotel Corporation, were forced to sell out. The Depression had taken its toll. The new owner was William Wrigley, the chewing-gum

66

The Arizona
Biltmore

Clark Gable putting at the hotel in 1940 (*above*) and an early game of lawn chess (*above right*).

magnate, who built himself a white stucco mansion with a Mediterranean barrel-tiled roof on a hillside overlooking the Biltmore. Frank Lloyd Wright attended a dinner party at Wrigley's home and is said to have muttered: "This house is an architect's desecration."

In the Wrigley era, the Biltmore was a hangout for Chicago and East Coast plutocrats, who pulled up beneath the jacaranda and citrus trees in their Cadillac limousines and stayed for the winter. If the rains came, they would hop on a plane to Palm Beach for a few days until the weather improved, but they always came back. They golfed, played cards, went horseback riding, and *always* dressed for dinner. One of the guests, Bill Goodman (of Bergdorf Goodman), appeared each evening throughout the season in a different dinner jacket.

Today's guests merely knot their ties, and sometimes not even that. Yet glamour at the Biltmore has not gone the way of steamer trunks. Under the current ownership of the Rostland Corporation, a Canadian investment group, and under the management of Westin Hotels, the Biltmore retains its elegant veneer.

The showplace for the high life at the Biltmore is the Orangerie restaurant, a dramatic peach and lime salon where the cascading chandeliers are shaped to look like stalactites. One evening during the dinner hour, an Orangerie waiter serves an hors d'ouevre of pickled, salmon-tinted quail eggs in an edible basket of fried potato slivers. A few hours later, as his diners prepare to depart, he presents a platter of giant, Hieronymous Bosch strawberries dipped in white chocolate. Both are gratis. In another corner of the room, a sommelier takes an order for Le Paradis, a rare, 1880 vintage cognac that sells for about $55 per glass. In the splendid center of things, Giovanni Messina, the maître d', welcomes special guests by personally whipping up his favorite fettucine recipe at a tableside cart.

Later that evening, the diners stroll the length of the cavernous rectangular lobby before settling down at the piano bar at the far end for a brandy. The famous recessed lights, a Frank Lloyd Wright trademark, cast a romantic glow.

Over by the front door, a bellboy stamps A.B., the Biltmore logo, in the sand in the two big pottery ashtrays.

The next morning, the Biltmore is at its resort best. Despite the austere architecture and sophisticated veneer, the hotel is a cheerful place. The Queen Anne palms on its lawns soften the bleakness of the concrete blocks, and 55 gardeners keep the grounds vibrant with snapdragons, pansies, peonies, amaryllis, and roses. Joggers pound the path beside the canals that weave around the grounds. (The canals were built alongside those originally dug by the extinct Hohokam Indians.) Golfers bid the runners good morning as they head the short distance from the hotel to the course. If the hour is right, a handful of hikers, including an occasional Biltmore guest, can be seen in the distance taking a morning climb up the jagged face of Squaw Peak.

Biltmore visitors come from all over the United States to explore the desert, brush up on their tennis and golf, and forget about business. (The hotel's brokerage office, with a ticker tape and full-size board, is long gone, though requests for stock reports are swiftly answered.) Increasingly, Europeans are visiting the Biltmore. The French rush into the shops to buy golf and tennis clothes, and can be overheard asking about American sizes. The English sometimes amuse the management by ordering afternoon tea. "*Nobody* drinks hot tea in the middle of a Phoenix afternoon," mutters a staffer.

68

The Arizona Biltmore

Most of the guests spend the afternoon lying around the pretty pool, which is lined with tiles from California's Catalina Island. Sipping strawberry margaritas under the palms, playing cards in front of the cabanas, they toast to a golden bronze. Now and then, the more energetic vacationers will walk past the bathers on their way to the health club, where regularly scheduled calisthenics classes are held. Many local Phoenix women also frequent the club, which has the distinction of having helped shape America's first female Supreme Court justice, Arizona's Sandra Day O'Connor. "You *knew* she was special," recalls Anne Kinnerup, director of the women's health club. Kinnerup has also supervised the stretching and bending of visiting celebrities like Joan Kennedy and Ava Gardner.

At the end of the day, the pool area is sometimes closed for a party, generally for one of the conference groups at the hotel. Women in white slacks and pastel tops or flowered cotton dresses (such as the ones modeled that noon at the luncheon fashion show) mill about with their spouses. The conversation is low key: the excellent weather, the golf, the advantages of Phoenix over the Caribbean. One night, reports a staffer, two men huddled by a striped beach umbrella discussing their plans to purchase a small European country.

At other moments, Biltmore guests gather for more exotic entertainment. The hotel believes that pampering its clientele means more than finding someone a fourth for bridge or studs for his shirtfront. (When *that* request came in, a bellboy was immediately dispatched to downtown Phoenix to buy the missing studs.) Pampering also means offering guests activities they can't get at home. Hot-air ballooning over the desert can be arranged on a few minutes' notice, as can a stagecoach ride in a vehicle equipped with a full bar, a television set, and a car engine. Steak fries and barbecues are popular diversions, too. At one barbecue, a band of Indians came whooping in on horseback. Upon closer inspection, the discerning guest could recognize members of the hotel staff slathered with makeup. When Merrill Lynch requested a bullfight for employees attending a conference at the Biltmore, the hotel built a corral and rounded up a bull.

Despite all these activities, the real lure of the Biltmore for many guests remains the extraordinary architecture and design. To preserve the hotel's unique heritage, the Biltmore has asked the Frank Lloyd Wright Foundation's Taliesin West in Scottsdale to supervise all new construction. Old or new, the architecture reflects the surroundings. The colors used predominantly in the public rooms are soft corals and lime greens, which evoke the glow of the mountains at sunset and the striking growth of the nearby cactus: saguaro, prickly pear, and staghorn. In the rooms, the same melons and limes and a few bolder blues and pinks swirl together through the draperies and bedspreads (in abstract patterns based on Frank Lloyd Wright designs). Here and there is a desk or table of etched bronze the color of the fading desert light. In the corridors of the older wings of the hotel, the walls are constructed of the same Biltmore blocks. These, according to Arnold Roy, Taliesin's project architect for the Biltmore, were Wright's way of reflecting the barrenness of the surrounding desert. In the geometric shapes in the blocks, explains Roy, Wright was mirroring the lush foliage of a desert oasis. "Mr. Wright's philosophy was to render nature architecturally," says Roy, his disciple. "He termed nature the only face of God we will ever see."

70

The Arizona Biltmore

Orangerie restaurant.

24th Street and Missouri
Phoenix, Arizona   85016

Telephone
602-955-6600

On the Premises: The Biltmore is a large resort with 500 rooms, 73 suites, and 12 small cottages. Two PGA golf courses with resident and teaching pros are within walking distance of the hotel. The resort also has 17 hard-surface tennis courts and 1 clay court, 3 pools, lawn bowling, shuffleboard, and a health club with steam, sauna, and massages. Riding is available at a nearby stable.

Rooms: Accommodations at the Biltmore vary widely in size, from the smaller rooms in the original part of the hotel to lavish, 600-feet suites. Each is furnished slightly differently. The colors are bold melons, oranges, turquoises, hot pinks, and greens; the fabrics are often abstracts based on Frank Lloyd Wright's designs. In the new Terrace Court wing, the oversize baths are accented with turquoise and gold stained-glass windows patterned with a Wright design (the shower mats match). Approximately two-thirds of the rooms have balconies or patios, and many have mini-bars. Other touches in the rooms include collapsible clotheslines in the tub, Alpha Keri soap and Vidal Sassoon shampoo, huge walk-in closets, and color television. The Persian suite is furnished with its own Gulbransen piano, the Bougainvillea suite has a sunken living room.

Meals: The Biltmore's showpiece is the Orangerie restaurant, open for lunch and dinner. The food, frequently cooked on tableside carts with great fanfare, is French and Continental (shrimp with fennel and Pernod, sweetbreads with pâté de fois gras, breast of chicken stuffed with lobster, veal medallions with crab royal). A second restaurant, the Gold Room, offers a table d'hôte and an a la carte menu that is less elaborate than that of the Orangerie. At breakfast and lunch, the Gold Room presents an enormous buffet as well as an a la carte selection. The Good Arizona Morning menu reflects the state's proximity to California, spiritually and physically. There are special vitamin- and energy-filled drinks like the Jogger (fresh papaya, orange juice, honey, egg and nutmeg) and Breakpoint (blueberries, pineapple juice, apple juice, and cream). The Biltmore is well known in Phoenix for its fine wine lists, which include excellent California "boutique" wines generally unavailable outside the state.

Getting There: Phoenix Sky Harbor International Airport is about 20 minutes by cab from the hotel, and pickup service is available on request. In this sprawling desert city, a car is helpful. If driving from the airport, take 24th Street north about 10 miles. Look for the hotel's sign on the right at 24th and Missouri.

Money Matters: The Biltmore is on the European plan but will offer modified and full American-plan rates and special packages on request. On the European plan high season rates (January 3 to May 29) range from $145 to $200 per double room. The hotel accepts all major credit cards.

Side Trips: Phoenix has an excellent zoo with 1,200 animals, a desert botanical garden, and Camelback Mountain, with wonderful views of the city and desert. Nearby Scottsdale, which bills itself as "the West's most Western town," is packed with boutiques and art galleries selling Indian and Southwestern art and artifacts. Farther afield, the famed Red Rock country near Flagstaff, the Grand Canyon

71

72

**The Arizona
Biltmore**

(the air tour over the canyon is a must), and Sunset Crater, a dormant volcano so named for the rainbow of molten rock and cinder on its cone, can all be visited on day trips arranged by the hotel.

Observations: Keep in mind that the hotel does a thriving conference business, and that five or more groups may be in residence at the same time. Because the resort is so large, however, the groups do not generally crowd the lobby or dining rooms. A self-contained conference center helps keep business gatherings unobtrusive. Also, remember that the Biltmore, by virtue of its size, can be a rather impersonal place. The staff, young and enthusiastic, compensates with warm and considerate service.

10 *The Arizona Inn*

Tucson, Arizona

In 1540 the mightly conquistador Francisco Vasquez de Coronado thundered through Tucson in search of the seven cities of gold. Clad in armor, he stood beneath the seering desert sun and scanned the terrain. Convinced that nothing in these parts glittered, he eventually led his armies on. But Coronado, look again. Over there by the swimming pool, an Arab in flowing robes gazes at the sunset. Over there on the patio, two weary movie stars, Gilda Radner and Gene Wilder, sip drinks under the palm trees after a day of filming the movie *Hanky Panky*.

The setting is The Arizona Inn, a pink adobe resort that probably would have shut its doors on Coronado and his boys (too rowdy) but clearly welcomes and caters to discriminating guests. The hotel has an air of low-key elegance for those who value anonymity at a price. "Do they know who I am?" wondered Gilda Radner when staff members carefully avoided asking for her autograph. Long before Radner's time, the reclusive Howard Hughes leased a cottage on the premises for seven years. Naturally, no one ever saw him lounging about. Some folks swear he merely kept the cottage in reserve, never staying there. Yet another regular, John D. Rockefeller, Jr., was a visible presence at the inn. He and Mrs. Rockefeller loved to motor around the countryside in a rented Cadillac limousine. "Mrs. Rockefeller enjoyed driving, so the chauffeur sat in back," recalls Assistant Manager Maynard Pike, who has been on staff since 1951. "They would go off into the desert, set up a card table, and have a picnic. They liked chicken salad with all white meat."

For families like the Rockefellers, The Arizona Inn was a novelty. On the edge of the desert sands, thousands of miles from proper Eastern civilization, the inn was nevertheless a place of decorum. When it first opened in 1930, Tucson was little more than a rough cow and copper town. The fledgling University of Arizona, a mile or so from the inn, put up a brick wall to keep out the roaming horses and cattle. At the inn, however, guests were coddled, and the servants who accompanied them were also well cared for. In fact, the inn's registration card still has a space for "maid, valet, or chauffeur." Today, the space generally remains blank, and the upstairs servants quarters have been converted into dainty guest bedrooms with white crewel spreads and antique prints on the walls.

Instead of servants, most guests bring their tennis rackets, a good book, and their spouse. The Arizona Inn is known as a quiet, romantic getaway for couples who want to brush up on their backhand, explore the desert, and get reacquainted with each other after the rigors of life back home.

The inn is the kind of place that sneaks up on the visitor. As one drives through an elegent residential area of Tucson, suddenly there it is, a splash of pink practically hugging the curb. No winding driveway or signs announce its presence. Discreet, even modest, it is shaded by olive trees. A yucca palm sways in front of the inn's major concession to pizazz: delft blue shutters that contrast boldly with the pink.

Inside the lobby, the visitor enters a world of cool white stucco walls and tasteful accents of color. A lithograph entitled *Blue Crane or Heron*, after J. J. Audubon, brightens one wall, and a European tapestry of a hunting scene adorns another. Suddenly, a cacophony of rapid-fire French breaks the silence. Two Parisian couples who have driven together across America to see the desert spread out their maps. One of the inn's regulars, a white-haired Northern woman who spends four months there each winter, looks up from her chair. Only last week she saw two Arabs in full regalia who stayed at the inn while they discussed desert-farming techniques with experts at the University of Arizona. (Because the terrain of Arizona and the Middle East are so similar, there is an ever-increasing flow of Arabs who visit the university to discuss agronomy.)

Cosmopolitan in its clientele, the inn is also eclectic in its decor. The Audubon Bar, a popular predinner gathering spot, looks like a set from a Humphrey Bogart movie with its bamboo chairs, hanging arrowhead philodendrons, and giant fishtail palm brushing the ceiling. On the walls are nine hand-colored J. J. Audubon lithographs from the 1840s. Nearby, in the so-called Catlin Dining Room, the walls are hung with 20 plates from American artist George Catlin's famed North American Indian portfolio. The adjacent African Room contains a display of carved wooden animals and weapons brought back to the inn from a safari. In the main dining room, a large white salon accented with pink table cloths, simple ladder-back chairs contrast with an imposing French gilt mirror and a Louis XV walnut armoire. The five-piece silver tea and coffee service tucked in a corner is American Federal. The collector of all this was Mrs. Isabella Greenway, the founder and longtime proprietress of the inn. Besides being an innkeeper with excellent taste, Mrs. Greenway was Arizona's first and, so far, only congresswoman.

She landed in the wilds of Arizona in the early part of the century via a circuitous route. The daughter of a Kentucky rancher, Isabella was sent to private school in Manhattan, where a classmate was Anna Eleanor Roosevelt. Isabella was a bridesmaid at Eleanor's marriage to Franklin Delano Roosevelt and, at nineteen, married a friend of Teddy Roosevelt's, a Scotsman named Robert Monroe Ferguson. Widowed in her twenties, she married Colonel John Greenway, a mining engineer who became a major force in Arizona politics.

Four years later, widowed once again, Isabella wandered through the West in a 1924 Packard touring car with her three children. "My mother realized that wasn't the right thing to do," recalls her daughter, Mrs. Charles Breastead, of Tucson. "So she bought a house in Tucson." Settled at last, she grew interested in the problems of World War I veterans. "She saw that they were in trouble," explains Mrs. Breasted. "So she gave them things like copper ashtrays, wooden toys, cactus canes, and lingerie bags for traveling, and told them that if they would copy them, she would try to sell them." Soon Mrs. Greenway encouraged her veterans to copy furniture. She opened a factory and showroom called The Arizona Hut, and quickly found herself operating a thriving business.

Then came the Depression. Furniture piled high in the factory, and Mrs. Greenway began furnishing her home with it. The beds and chests kept stacking up. Eventually, after filling a few cottages with the veterans' handiwork, she opened an inn. It was the middle of the Depression. Yet Mrs. Greenway felt that the Arizona climate would lure certain types of persons from the East. "She built great big closets and big rooms for Easterners," says her daughter. "She knew their life-style."

The provident Mrs. Greenway also knew something local entrepreneurs would learn much later: that the sunny, dry Tucson climate is a balm to chilly Easterners. As the tourists flocked to her resort, Mrs. Greenway headed to Washington in 1933 to make her entry into politics. She served in Congress until 1936, when she retired "to give a little time to my family." Until her death in 1953, Mrs. Greenway also kept a close eye on the inn. Under the ownership of her son, John Selmes Greenway, it remains largely as she would have

76

The Arizona Inn

wanted. The rooms are still furnished with the light maple tables and sleigh beds crafted by her veterans.

Visiting the inn is like stepping back into a quieter era. Beyond the main building are lush gardens and winding walkways that lead to clusters of pink stucco cottages, each with its own patio. Beds of snapdragons, poppies, and anemones are tended by a platoon of gardeners. Orange trees, native cypress, and date palms shade the grass, reseeded twice a year to keep it the proper hue of green. At the end of one walkway is an enormous swimming pool, protected on one side by a trellis for those who don't like the strong Tucson sun.

As the sun drops low over the desert, the action shifts to the library, a baronial room with a vaulted ceiling, or to the shaded patio. The library appears to be the preserve of the inn's "social guests," a loyal cadre of rather elderly ladies who gather for a card game and a chat. Out on the patio, a younger crowd sips margaritas and watches the orange glow of sunset. Later, after a candlelit dinner, they will wash off the crumbs in silver finger bowls. They might take a walk through the gardens before finally climbing into a vintage sleigh bed. It is said that Howard Hughes even tried to purchase his bed, and learned that at last he had stumbled upon something money couldn't buy. But in the true spirit of Mrs. Greenway's hospitality, the management gladly "loaned" him one for his cottage behind the palms.

77

2200 East Elm
Tucson, Arizona   85719

Telephone
602-325-1541

On the Premises: Located in a quiet, residential area of Tucson, the inn has 85 rooms and 7 suites. It offers guests two clay tennis courts, a large heated pool, a putting green, croquet, and table tennis. Golf can be arranged at a nearby club, and horseback riding at a Tucson stable.

Rooms: Most accommodations are unusually spacious and have color televisions, large closets, and private patios. Each room is decorated differently with 1930s sleigh beds and antiques. Room 154, for example, has a Victorian lampstand with spool-turned legs, four decorative bird prints on the walls, an adobe fireplace, and a crimson flowered spread and drapes. Another especially pretty accommodation is suite 133, which has a pink and blue sitting room and lithographs of menacing Chippewa and Creek Indian chiefs on the walls.

Meals: Silver finger bowls are served after every meal (breakfast, too); the china is pink and blue with birds of the area strutting across the plates, and the service is friendly and attentive. At breakfast, order a Danish and it will be presented with a flourish beneath a silver-domed warmer. Or, try eggs Florentine, or perhaps a Western omelet with green chili. At lunch, crab, shrimp, and fruit salads are on the menu, as well as heartier dishes like baked beans, corned-beef hash and eggs, and barbecued ribs. The evening menu, which changes frequently, is Continental (salmon with pecan butter; brochette of beef with Bordelaise sauce; boneless trout with crab, and veal stuffed with lobster). The standout dessert is the inn's mud pie, a concoction of coffee ice cream, butterscotch sauce, whipped cream, and chopped nuts in a crust made from crushed Oreo cookies.

Getting There: The inn is about 20 minutes by taxi from the Tucson Airport. Driving from the direction of the airport, take Interstate 10 to the Speedway exit; turn right off the exit and then left on Campbell and right on Elm. Continue down Elm to the inn.

Money Matters: A room at the inn is generally on the European plan, though a full American plan can be arranged. On the European plan, a double room begins at $55 in the low season (May 1 to October 1) and can run as high as $81. From October 1 to December 31, doubles range from $78 to $85. High-season rates (January 1 to April 30) are $74 to $105 per double room. Suites, of course, are more expensive. The inn accepts MasterCard, Visa, and American Express.

Side Trips: The Arizona-Sonora Desert Museum, 14 miles west of town, provides a superb orientation to the desert. In the Coronado National Forest, an open-air tram carries visitors along a winding road up and down Sabino Canyon. The San Xavier Mission is worth a visit, as is Tucson's Old Town, which has authentic stagecoach rides, five gunfights daily, and a journey through the Iron Door Mine. Bird watchers should visit Madera Canyon and Ramsey Canyon.

Observations: The inn is a quiet, rather stately place that caters to a fairly subdued clientele. Although it has well-maintained recreational facilities, it is not for the traveler who demands round-the-clock resort facilities. Its appeal is in its ambience, lush gardens, attentive service, and unique history.

11 *The Broadmoor*

Colorado Springs, Colorado

In the dark days of Prohibition, a dapper, mustachioed gentleman managed to intoxicate the population of Colorado Springs with his antics. Spencer Penrose, Spec, to the locals, traveled about town in a cart pulled by a llama. With all eyes upon him, he colorfully protested the government's ban on booze. Whether or not the peregrinations of Penrose had much effect on the repeal of Prohibition may never be known. Of his contribution to the liquor industry, there is little doubt: encased behind glass at The Broadmoor are rows and rows of bottles (empty) stockpiled in dry days by the perspicacious Mr. Penrose. Wide ranging in his tastes, Spec amassed everything from an 1869 Jerez sherry and a 1903 Château Lafite to an undated specimen marked "Doctor's Special Liqueur Cream of superior flavour and good quality guaranteed pre-war strength."

The legends — and legacy — of Penrose persist at The Broadmoor, the shell-pink resort he founded in 1918 at the foot of the Rockies. A blueblood from Philadelphia, Penrose headed West in the 1890s and joined the gold rush at Cripple Creek. He later helped found the Utah Copper Company, which was in turn bought by the Kennecott Copper Corporation in 1923. The adventurous Penrose then turned his copper cash into the finer things in life. Many years after his death, the vestiges of his eclectic taste, not only in alcohol but also in art and architecture, linger on at The Broadmoor.

The hotel was the dream of Penrose and his cultured, Detroit-born wife, Julie Villiers Lewis McMillan Penrose. Strolling through Colorado Springs on their regular walks, gazing at the spectacle of Pikes Peak 12 miles in the distance, Spec and Julie got builder's itch. Again and again they returned to the lakeside site of an old hotel and casino. The Penroses fell in love with the setting and the notion of building a grand hotel such as the ones they had seen in their wanderings through Europe. They purchased the property, arranged to have the hotel and casino moved (the hotel is now gone and the casino is the golf club), and hired the New York firm of Warren and Wetmore to design a new resort. As construction proceeded, both Penroses paid close attention to detail. In her book *The Broadmoor Story*, historian Helen Geiger notes that Mrs. Penrose concerned herself with all the furnishing and decoration, "even the shelves in the linen closet." Mr. Penrose, Geiger writes, "was not above such matters as personally choosing the bathroom fixtures, insisting upon seeing samples before he would place an order."

In 1918 The Broadmoor was finally ready to receive callers. Guestes invited to the opening night party — "the big blowout," as Penrose called it — arrived to

The Penrose Suite (*above*) and a view of the mountain landscape (*above right*).

find a theatrical, Mediterranean-style hotel with a slender bell tower and a red barrel-tiled roof. They marveled at the frescoes and bas-reliefs created by a small army of artisans imported from Italy. They danced on the marble floors beneath gold-leaf chandeliers and dined on velouté de volaille, braised sweetbreads aux perles du Perigord, boneless royal squab, and souffle glacé Cômtesse de Cornet.

Over the years The Broadmoor grew even more lavish. The Penroses added antiques purchased on their travels abroad and landscaped the grounds with gardens and hanging baskets filled with marigolds, snapdragons, and sweet alyssum. Inside the walls of the quaint porte cochere, Mr. Penrose hung the heads of buffalo, Rocky Mountain sheep, a deer, and other trophies. The centaurs frolicked in the Carrara-marble fountain a few steps away, seemingly indifferent to this new wildlife.

The guests, then and now, were delighted. The original Broadmoor has become the nucleus of a large resort incorporating three separate hotels on a private lake, a conference center, pools, tennis courts, a world-famous championship skating rink, three golf courses, and its own ski slope. It is owned by the El Pomar Investment Company, a subsidiary of the El Pomar Foundation (a charitable organization set up by Spencer Penrose). A city unto itself (it has actually been so at times in its history), The Broadmoor has its own power plant, greenhouse, garage, and post office. With its various facilities, the resort attracts a broad range of guests. In the fall through the spring, it is enormously popular with conference groups, which find the proper mix of business and pleasure at The Broadmoor. In the summer The Broadmoor becomes a family hotel. Kids paddle across the lake in bright yellow boats. Their parents watch from the shore, sometimes feeding the ducks and Canadian geese that waddle up and down the banks. Bicyclists pedal along the narrow path that winds around the water. Over at the skating arena, a mother watches as her eight-year-old daughter practices a credible figure eight. Inside Julie's, an ice-cream

81

parlor on the premises named after Mrs. Penrose, a half-dozen kids who met that afternoon at the pool are knocking off sundaes.

That evening, after the children are asleep, some of their parents will gather in the Golden Bee, a seventeenth-century English pub with gingerbread trim that was moved from England to New York, and later found a home at The Broadmoor's conference center (called the International Center). In the glow of its old-fashioned gaslight-type fixtures, they will sing to a honky-tonk piano and drink yards of ale.

The Golden Bee is the hotel's concession to old-time Colorado, when everybody gathered in Victorian saloons. The rest of the resort is a touch of Europe (Asia, too) in the Rockies. Each of the three hotels has its own personality and facilities, including lobby, dining rooms, and shops. The grand doyenne remains the original Broadmoor, now called Broadmoor Main. Stepping into its lobby is like arriving at an elegant hotel on the shores of Italy's Lake Como. Crystal chandeliers light its textured crimson walls and handsome oak trim. A travertine marble staircase spirals upward to sun-rooms and parlors filled with French and Italian furniture—and a few curiosities. In the so-called Fireplace Room, for example, a nude gentleman with two left feet dances on the bas-relief ceiling. A Maxfield Parrish oil of The Broadmoor, commissioned in 1919, depicts the hotel on the wrong side of the lake—for reasons no one seems to know. Nearby, in the main dining room, the original grand salon during the Penrose era, gold cherubs hold up lamps; the smoked mirrors and gold moldings give the feel of a Renaissance drawing room. The crowd sitting there one morning at breakfast was a respectably well-dressed bunch: sport coats and ties and an occasional golf outfit on the men, tailored dresses on the women. (The pink and green pants one sees at many sports-minded resorts are largely absent at The Broadmoor.)

Just south of the Broadmoor Main is the Broadmoor South. Constructed in 1961, it has the same soft pink exterior, red tile roof, and Mediterranean feeling. In fact, the architects closely modeled it on the earlier hotel next door. Inside, the rather small, marble-floored lobby looks like that of an elegant European pension. Dominating the lobby is a crimson tapestry of the original Broadmoor, with the somber-faced Spencer Penrose in the foreground. Seven floors above is yet another tribute to Spec, the Penrose Room, one of the most popular dining rooms at the resort. Here, the views are excellent. The setting is a cross between a French court and a Greek temple. The chairs are Louis XV, the china collection Napoleonic, and the wallpaper an eighteenth-century hand-screened pattern. But in various spots, cherubs dance on delicate Greek tapers.

The refined grace of the Broadmoor South and Main appeals to Europeans, older couples, and family groups with a reverence for the past. The newest hotel in the complex, the Broadmoor West, seems to attract a slightly younger crowd. Its pink walls and red roof mirror its sister hotels. Similarities end there. Set apart from the others on the far side of the lake, Broadmoor West is angular and modern, with tiered balconies facing the mountains. Inside its lobby one has left Italy and France and arrived in the Orient. This is where the Penroses housed their collection of Asian art. Quan'n yin, a 10-foot-high stone goddess of mercy, stares coolly at visitors. The 300-year-old bronze temple dogs guard the comings and goings of the guests.

A walk down the corridor and the scene shifts again. Now, one is in the dining room of an English manor house: the Charles Court, which some say is the best dining room in the resort. Settle down here in front of the graceful windows draped with chintzes and watch the squirrels and geese by the lake.

Against this imposing backdrop, guests spend long hours reading on the terraces overlooking the lake and leisurely walking its circumference (slightly under a mile around). The more athletic head for one of the three championship golf courses, where the resident pro is Dow Finsterwald. Playing a mountain course, he'll tell you, can be tricky. "The mountains create an illusion," he explains, "You think you're hitting uphill, and actually you're hitting down."

The mountain air has long attracted skaters to these parts. The Broadmoor World Arena is famous as a training ground for skaters. "It's the Wimbledon of skating." says Carlo Fassi, the director of skating and the man who instructed Peggy Fleming, John Curry, and Robin Cousins. (Fleming trained at The Broadmoor from 1965 to 1969.) The arena is also the site of figure-skating, hockey, and curling championships, as well as ice reviews and Pops on Ice. Broadmoor guests can watch the events and participate in skating sessions.

Over the years the attractions of The Broadmoor have drawn many celebrated visitors. Archduke Otto of Austria, King Hussein of Jordan, the king of Siam, Igor Stravinsky, Herbert Hoover, and Dwight Eisenhower have all come to call. A favorite Broadmoor anecdote dates from the time John Wayne was in residence. He decided he wanted to slip up to his room unnoticed, so he took the service elevator. His fellow passenger was a young waiter bringing a platter of iced shrimp up to a suite. The Duke promptly ate all the shrimp, shoved a $20 bill in the waiter's pocket, and said "Thanks, kid" as he sauntered off at his floor. Another Hollywood type, Joan Crawford, sent a three-page list of instructions in advance of her arrival stipulating, among other things, that "Miss Crawford is a star and should be treated like a star."

All the famous guests, presumably, came away with happy memories. But Mr. and Mrs. J. C. Penney were virtually ecstatic. They arrived for a 22-day stay in 1967 and ordered a double portion of oysters on the half shell every night. One evening, as Mrs. Penney dug into her oyster, she found, yes, a pearl. Even when it doles out unintended souvenirs, The Broadmoor does it in style.

83

PO Box 1439
Colorado Springs, Colorado ·80901

Telephone
303-634-7711

On the Premises: The Broadmoor is a large and luxurious resort consisting of three separate hotels, the genteel Broadmoor Main and Broadmoor South, and the more modern Broadmoor West. Together, the hotels contain 560 rooms and 60 suites. The resort offers three 18-hole championship golf courses, skeet and trapshooting, fishing, and year-round ice skating. From Thanksgiving through March, The Broadmoor provides skiing at Ski Broadmoor on nearby Cheyenne Mountain; the area has two trails serviced by a double chair lift and features night skiing under powerful floodlights.

Rooms: By far, the most modern accommodations at The Broadmoor are at Broadmoor West. The rooms are spacious, with separate makeup areas, huge closest with removable wooden hangers and a full-length mirror, and balconies overlooking the lake. Each has a refrigerator, color television, push-button phone, unobtrusive carved oak furniture, and simple, subtly patterned fabrics. In the baths are piles of fluffy towels, a marble-topped vanity, and a supply of bubble bath, Neutrogena soap, bath oil, and shampoo. Accommodations in Broadmoor South and Main vary widely; they are generally decorated with floral prints and chintzes. For a splurge, ask for the Penrose Suite, where Mrs. Julie Penrose lived her last days. Its three bedrooms, solarium, and two sitting rooms reflect the Penroses' eclectic tastes: eighteenth-century French furniture, Oriental chests and silk screens, floral draperies and spreads, and a collection of old crystal. The view from the solarium stretches 10 miles over the town of Colorado Springs.

84

The Broadmoor

The hotel's ski resort on
Cheyenne Mountain.

Meals: Breakfast is served in the main dining room or in the Charles Court, where filet of Rocky Mountain trout and oysters Orly (fried in beer batter and presented on Canadian bacon) are on the menu along with eggs Benedict and silver-dollar-size pancakes. Lunch might be crepes or corned beef on Russian rye in the Tavern, where the walls are covered with Toulouse-Lautrecs; a sandwich and sundae in Julie's ice-cream parlor; or a more elaborate meal in the Penrose Room or Charles Court. Casual dinners are available at the Tavern, Julie's, and the Golden Bee. For a special supper, order caviar, broiled lobster tails, or perhaps chateaubriand with Béarnaise sauce in the Penrose Room; in the Charles Court, try the quenelles of Dover sole, the maître d's special pressed duck, or Rocky Mountain trout selected from the aquarium at the front of the room.

Getting There: The Colorado Springs Airport is a 15-minute trip from the hotel by taxi. If driving from the north or south, take Interstate 25 to the Harrison exit, then turn west; the road leads directly to the hotel. From east or west, take Interstate 24 to 21st Street, then go south to the end of the road and right at The Broadmoor.

Money Matters: The price of a double room on the European plan ranges from $75 to $105 from November to May and $115 to $155 from May to November. The Broadmoor issues its own credit card to frequent visitors, but accepts no commercial credit cards.

Side Trips: A cog railway (owned and operated by The Broadmoor) makes the round trip to the summit of Pikes Peak in 3 hours, 10 minutes. At the top (chilly in any season and very cold in winter), on a clear day one can see north to Denver, 75 miles away, and south to the Sangre de Cristo Mountains of New Mexico. The area also offers visitors the attractions of the Cheyenne Mountain Zoo, a mountain shrine dedicated to humorist Will Rogers; sandstone rock formation; and the U.S. Air Force Academy.

Observations: This is an enormous resort that offers sports facilities, accommodations, and cuisine for every taste. It does a thriving conference business from fall to spring. The Broadmoor is not for those seeking a small, romantic hideaway.

85

12 *Tall Timber*

Durango, Colorado

This is a resort distinguished for what it *doesn't* have. Built on a former potato field 7,550 feet up in Colorado's San Juan National Forest, Tall Timber is sans telephone (guests are discouraged from using the management's radio phone), television, radio, room service, a set menu, dancing, horseback riding, even locked doors.

But wait. Keep reading. Tall Timber offers a mountain isolation so complete that one guest called it an aphrodisiac. It also has salves for the sybarite. Maids tiptoe into the duplex cabins secluded behind aspen groves to lay fresh kindling in the fireplaces and chocolates (shaped like pinecones) on the pillows. The chef serves everything from kiwis to caviar in a candlelit dining room. Hot tubs bubble on a redwood deck. Then, too, there is a Finnish sauna, an 80-degree swimming pool with curved slide, a tennis court, even a shallow spot in the river where one can attempt to pan for gold.

To the Tall Timber clientele, who reserve, as one generally must, about 6 to 12 months in advance, the greatest lure is the sensation of being both a pampered guest and a pioneer. "At this point in my life, I'm rather spoiled," says a woman from Houston. "I like to go hiking, but I don't want to carry a backpack and eat dried beef stew. It's nice to be able to come back, sit in the whirlpool, and have a lovely dinner. When you return to your room at night, the towels are fresh and the bed is turned down. What more could one want?"

Some guests selectively forget all these niceties in the retelling back home. "We're antisnobs," says a teacher from Illinois. "We want our friends to think we're roughing it." As she speaks, she lolls lazily in a poolside chair digesting that day's lunch of hot tomato bouillon, buttermilk biscuits, chicken crepes, and homemade brandy wafers filled with whipped cream. Her businessman husband, content but sending out faint signals of wanderlust, mumbles something about wishing he could take a drive.

That he can't. There are no roads leading to Tall Timber. The only access is by helicopter or the lone railroad track running the 45-mile distance between Durango and Silverton, two old-fashioned Western towns. (Tall Timber is about halfway between them.) The coal-powered steam engine that grinds up the mountainous track is not just any train, mind you. It is the last regularly scheduled narrow-gage railroad in the United States. Cinder-ella, as Hollywood called her when she starred (along with Robert Redford and Paul Newman) in the movie *Butch Cassidy and the Sundance Kid*, was constructed in 1881. In those days she hauled gold, silver, magnesium, and iron from the mines of Silverton to the smelter in Durango.

Today the mines are closed, but the tourists could care less as they ride this relic from a bygone era. The adventure begins in Durango, a Wild West – style town with wide streets swirling with dust, gaslight restaurants, and saloons. Most Tall Timber guests spend a night in Durango before climbing aboard the morning train. With a great spurt of steam, the black locomotive pulls out of the depot. As the *Silverton*, as she is called, clatters through the outskirts of town and into the hills, her mustard yellow cars snake around curves. Tourists hang out the windows, cameras aimed at the fields of columbine. Soon waterfalls and hot springs come into sight as the train clings confidently to a cliff 1,000 feet above the churning waters of the Animas River.

This river valley is called El Cañón Del Rio de Las Animas Perdidas (The Canyon of the River of the Lost Souls). It was here, according to legend, that an expedition of priests, soldiers, and Indians searching for a trade route between Santa Fe and California lost their lives. A mutiny in the ranks followed by the bitter Colorado winter wiped out the entire party. Later, a Spanish explorer sent out to find them discovered the bodies and concluded that the men had died without receiving the last rites of the Catholic Church. He gave the valley its haunting name. Sometimes, when the wind is right, say the locals, you can hear the lost souls crying in the night.

On the train, the loudest sounds are the wheels, whistles, and exclamations from the passengers. Two hours or so into the journey, the train halts in front of a chocolate-brown depot. The brakemen, husky, handsome, and straight out of Central Casting in their denim overalls, usher the Tall Timber guests off the *Silverton*.

"Welcome to Tall Timber," says owner Dennis Beggrow. Denny and his wife, Judy, are modern-day pioneers. In 1970, newly married and determined to carve out an independent life for themselves, they purchased a 180-acre tract of land, including an open meadow, along the railroad track. The flat, as they call it, is the largest level area in this mountainous forestland. Centuries ago, the Ute Indians had set up a summer hunting camp on the meadow. In the late 1880s, Chinese laborers working on the railroad built a still on the flat and brewed potato hooch. By the 1950s, the level expanse had become a popular movie site. Hollywood film directors had discovered that it was the only place along the track to get a good long shot of the Indians chasing the train. Hence, the site that was later to become Tall Timber is immortalized in movies like *Naked Spur, Ticket to Tomahawk*, and *Night Passage*.

Denny and Judy had long known about the flatland. Judy's parents owned a dude rance, Ah Wilderness, about a mile down the track. Denny and his family, who were in the hotel business in Florida, went there for vacations. "As a teenager, I had chased a lot of horses on this flat," recalls Denny. By the time he had graduated from the School of Hotel and Restaurant Management at the University of Denver and married Judy, the land was on the market.

The Beggrows bought it, camped out in tents, and began building their dream, a luxury resort. First came the essentials: water, electricity, and plumbing. Then, they built pine guest cabins and a lodge that housed a kitchen, a dining room with beamed valuted ceiling, and a library. Weary but proud, the Beggrows welcomed their first guests in 1974.

The current crop of adventurers who ride the rails to Tall Timber find a far more polished resort. Since 1976 the Beggrows have added the depot, which serves as an office and tiny shop, and a cabana area with hot tubs. They have also built more accommodations. While his staff (12 for the 24 or so guests Tall Timber can handle) efficiently sorts luggage and delivers it to the appropriate rooms, the proprietor of this hand-hewn hideaway takes all new arrivals on a leisurely stroll around the grounds. He points out the vegetable patches where his resident gardner, Janet Randall, cultivates most of the produce served in the

A Timber suite tucked in the woods.

89

The narrow-gage railway and Henry, the old 1932 Ford pickup truck, which is a Tall Timber fixture.

restaurant. Moving past the tennis court, Beggrow pauses by the swimming pool. The fiberglass pool is exactly 40 feet long by 6½ feet wide—the dimensions of a narrow-gage railroad flatcar. Denny had made three attempts to bring in a larger fiberglass shell by helicopter. Each time the shell plummeted to earth in one mishap or another. Finally, he gave up, ordered a mold that could be hauled up on the railroad, and installed his pool. "When we began all this," he remembers, "we knew there would be a lot of adversities. But we didn't think about them."

As his guests quietly take it all in, Beggrow then shows off the dining room. Its enormous fireplace is constructed of stones carted from a rockslide up the track. A wine rack is carved into the fireplace. Abstract wood chandeliers dangle above simple pine tables and high-backed leather chairs. In one corner, a spiral staircase leads up to a library stocked with 3,000 books.

Finally, Beggrow leads his guests across the flat and up a winding path to the cluster of cabins. The one-bedroom Timber suites and two-bedroom Timber hearths are a little like ski-country condominiums in feeling. Downstairs is a living room with wet bar, stone fireplace, and hide-a-bed sofa upholstered in a furry fabric. A traditional Navajo weaving decorates one wall. In the Timber suites, there is an upstairs sleeping loft with a queen-size bed and a bureau under a beamed cathedral ceiling. The Timber hearths have two separate bedrooms upstairs. All the baths are outfitted with stacks of fluffy towels and cocoa-butter soap. "So this is roughing it?" jokes a New Yorker who had clearly expected a cot and a few camp blankets.

The grand tour over, the guests unpack, then drift up to the dining room for lunch. There, the chef and the baker are preparing the day's damage. "The average weight gain is about 2 pounds per week," acknowledges John Haveles, Tall Timber's general manager. (The figure fluctuates, of course, with the amount of hiking and the number of desserts.) Each meal at the resort is a multicourse salvo of homemade soups, vegetables and salads from Janet's garden, freshly baked breads, imaginative entrees, and plenty of liqueur-laced desserts. "People get mad at me because I make them fat," admits Cheryl Beitz, Tall Timber's pastry chef. She also confides that a man from Denver celebrating his honeymoon at Tall Timber offered to take her back home.

The staff at Tall Timber are a loyal cadre who speak of the resort's isolation and beauty in terms that border on the religious. After a few days, most guests are also converts to the mountain life. "Being here, surrounded by all these trees and sky, I can forget about my problems," says a Texan. "Really? I find that all this makes me want to confront them and solve them," interjects a listener. That latter attitude seems most prevalent. Unable to call the office, to compulsively consume in souvenir shops, or to submerge one's troubles in television, the average guest turns inward. Couples find themselves really talking to one another. Children on vacation with their parents learn that they actually *like* them.

Tall Timber guests seem to divide into two distinct groups: the homebodies who hibernate in their suites and the sportsmen who play golf or tennis or don hiking boots each morning and, taking along a picnic lunch, head up into the aspen and spruce. They return in the late afternoon brandishing sprays of Indian paintbrush, larkspur, and buttercups. As the sun edges behind the trees, they settle down with something cool and wet. Nothing so crass as a bar with plastic stools and bowls of peanuts would *ever* exist at Tall Timber. A young waitress roams the property in a golf cart stocked with soda and alcohol and dispenses drinks wherever she is flagged down. Later in the evening, after dinner and perhaps a postprandial dip in the hot tubs, the guests drift off to their cabins. With no discotheque, formal bar, or Las Vegas – style band to detain them, most folks discover the pleasures of a good book in front of a fire.

This mountain solitude isn't for everybody. "A swinging single wouldn't like this type of vacation," cautions Denny. He has found that his happiest guests are strong-minded individualists who take pleasure in entertaining themselves. He has also discovered over the years that it is mostly women who initially seek out Tall Timber and make the reservations. "A woman is looking for a place where her husband will stop worrying about the business and get his pipe out," he reflects. "Yet she doesn't want to go to some fishing camp, wash his dirty socks, and clean the catch." At Tall Timber, she is served her husband's catch for breakfast, if she so desires. On fine china.

91

SSR Box 90
Durango, Colorado   81301

Telephone
303-259-4813

On the Premises: Remote, accessible only by railroad or helicopter, Tall Timber is a place to unwind and explore nature and one's feelings. The resort accommodates a maximum of 24 people in duplex cabins. "If you are dependent upon telephones, television, radio, or for some reason enjoy noise and air and water pollution, you may not find Tall Timber to your liking. We provide none of those things," says the management. They do provide endless marked game trails that weave along mountain streams and hot springs; trout fishing in the Animas River; tennis, swimming, hot tubs, a nine-hole, 29-par golf course, and a putting green.

Rooms: The accommodations, crafted from natural pine, cedar, and stone, are all fairly similar in style. The greens, browns, and rusts of the fabrics are the colors of the Tall Timber forest. Each woodsy one- or two-bedroom cabin has its own private deck and fireplace and a wet bar. Because Tall Timber does not sell liquor by the bottle, bring your own.

Meals: In its efforts to encourage total relaxation, Tall Timber believes its guests should do away with decision making. Hence, the kitchen staff offers no menu. Diners arrive at the appointed time and are presented with a multicourse feast that is entirely at the whim of the chef. Breakfast starts with fresh fruit and progresses to rye waffles served with heated maple syrup one day; another day might bring eggs Benedict on homemade English muffins and sour-cream coffee cake washed down with fresh papaya, pomegranate, or blackberry juice. A special breakfast favorite at Tall Timber is the airy puffed pancakes served with strawberries. Lunches are robust: vegetable quiches; pastrami on homemade bagels; hot roast beef with a French dip sauce served on a freshly baked hoagie; spicy manicotti. The evening meal, served by candlelight, is an elegant repast of classic French and Continental cuisine (mountain trout sautéed in almonds and expertly filleted at tableside; filet of beef Wellington with mushroom duxelles; veal Marsala or parmigiana with homemade linguini; prime ribs accompanied by a bouquet of homegrown vegetables). At every meal there is freshly baked bread, such as a braided anise loaf or sourdough, and an imaginative dessert, often flambéed at the table. The Tall Timber specialty is a sour-cream pound cake topped with vanilla ice cream and fresh blackberries and flamed with crème de cassis and applejack. The banana meringue pie, apple dumplings with rum sauce, and nutty cheesecake are also favorites. The wine list, small but carefully chosen, features moderately priced California and French wines. Most people find that in the high altitude one glass is the equivalent of two, and drink sparingly.

Getting There: This is definitely (almost) half the fun. There are no roads to Tall Timber, only a railroad track serviced by the Durango and Silverton Narrow Gage Railroad Company. The dramatic ride through spectacular mountain scenery takes about two hours. The trains generally leave early in the morning from Durango, and return in the late afternoon (schedules vary with the season). At the time one makes a reservation at Tall Timber, the management volunteers to obtain round-trip railroad tickets (a necessity since this popular tourist railroad is sometimes booked solid months in advance by people wanting to make the round-trip journey to Silverton). Tall Timber will also make reservations at a Durango hotel or motel for guests who plan to spend the night before or after their train trip in this vintage Western town. For those who want quicker transportation to Tall Timber, Rocky Mountain Helicopters makes the trip in 12 minutes. Tall Timber will help make reservations.

Money Matters: The management of Tall Timber believes that it takes time to adjust to the wilderness experience. It is best appreciated, they say, in a week's stay. During July, August, and September, Tall Timber generally accepts reservations by the week only; the rate in double accommodations is $720 per person, per week, including three meals a day. In May and early June and later in the fall, shorter stays are allowed at the rate of $150 per person, per night. Credit cards are not accepted.

Side Trips: Excursions are strictly by foot through aspen forests brilliant with mountain wild flowers. For the more adventurous, Tall Timber will arrange daylong fishing trips (by helicopter) to a mountain lake.

Observations: This is a vacation unlike any other. If you seek a lively resort with a wide range of activities, Tall Timber is not for you. What the resort *does* have is superb personal service, gourmet cuisine, and comfortable suites in the middle of the wilderness. Once one arrives at Tall Timber, there is no quick getaway (except by helicopter) if you don't like it. Nor is there the usual sightseeing or souvenir shops. Guests are encouraged to enjoy the beauties of the surroundings. More than a resort, it is a way of life. Be sure it is right for you.

93

13 *Inn of the Mountain Gods*

Mescalero, New Mexico

In the dusty canyons of southern New Mexico, the ghost of an Indian brave seen dangling from a fir tree when the moon is full seems no more or no less real than the three separate graves said to hold the bones of Billy the Kid. A guiding spirit high in the cobalt blue sky still whispers advice to the local medicine men and leads the Indian maidens through ancient puberty rites.

This sun-bleached land of legend and lore is the home of the Mescalero Apache, a tribe whose warriors once terrorized the Southwest. Not known for their hospitality, the Apache have nevertheless assumed the unexpected responsibility of owning and operating a modern resort hotel right on their 460,384-acre reservation. Inn of the Mountain Gods, a cedar chalet 7,000 feet up in a canyon of the Sacramento Mountains, is a tribute to Apache ingenuity and to the wisdom of tribal president Wendell Chino. "We have the altitude and the scenery here," says Chino. "I realized one day that if we didn't capitalize on our land, we could starve on it."

Under Chino's guidance, the Mescalero Apache opened a $22 million luxury hotel on tribal acres in 1975. The main lodge, seven connecting smaller lodges, and a new conference center all sprawl along the banks of man-made Lake Mescalero. On the far side of the water, in front of snowcapped Sierra Blanca, a sacred mountain to the Indians, stand two Apache tepees. "Just for show," chuckles an Indian staffer.

In its decor and design, the inn draws relatively modestly on its Indian heritage. Tucked in the mountains, surrounded by forests of pine, oak, aspen, fir, and juniper, it looks from the outside like a European ski lodge. The lobby, however, is warmed by a three-story copper-sheathed fireplace that narrows at the top like a tepee. A mountain spirit wearing headdress and moccasins, the symbol of the Mescalero Apache, dances on a plaque in the middle.

In the main dining room, the Indian baskets hanging on the walls and the elkhorn chandeliers are in stark contrast with the modern Breuer chairs. The Continental cuisine is served on white china edged with a colorful Zuni-inspired motif. The same pattern appears on the smocks worn by the waitresses.

To the guests, the real wonder of being fed and coddled in the middle of an Indian reservation comes from watching the Apache themselves. A handsome, rather bashful group, they are friendly but a little reserved. One of the more jocular is Melford Yuzas, an amiable man who takes visitors to the nearby Sierra Blanca Ski Resort (also owned and operated by the Mescalero). "Where did you learn to drive a bus?" asks a guest, who still harbors the impression

95

that Indians only ride horses. "From a white man," deadpans Melford, a lanky six-footer who strolls about in pointed-toe red-and-white tooled leather boots, jeans, a bandana, and a cowboy hat. The turquoise and abalone on the band signify his status as one of the tribe's seven medicine men.

At the inn's first-rate gift shop, Rita Chino, Wendell's wife, sells jewelry to perplexed visitors who aren't quite sure if New Mexico is part of the United States. Some want to know whether the shop accepts pesos or changes money. "Is it okay to drink the water here?" one man whispers conspiratorily as he purchases a turquoise-and-silver squash-blossom necklace for his wife. Mrs. Chino, who stocks her shop with some museum-quality necklaces and beads and silver concho belts, answers questions about the currency, the water, and the merchandise with cheerful aplomb.

Most of the Indians, in fact, are tolerant and understanding of the misperceptions visitors have about their life and their land. They even give their guests a real tribal show now and then. This takes place at the powwows staged periodically by the pool. On a warm evening, as the sun sets low over Sierra Blanca, the sounds of chanting and tom-toms echo across the lake. Indian women sit cross-legged outside brush arbors (ceremonial, igloo-shaped huts made of spruce saplings). They cook puffed fried bread in black iron skillets over open fires. Indian dancers in fringed buckskin perform an assortment of steps as their emcee moderates: "This dance commemorates our efforts to inspire fertility in the land . . ." To the hotel guests, it is a moment to be savored. Strolling about, tasting the bread, and sipping strawberry margaritas, they are delighted.

Each year around the Fourth of July, guests at the inn have the rare opportunity to witness parts of a sacred ceremony held on the reservation itself. This is the coming of age rite for Apache maidens. During the five ceremonial days, young girls who have reached puberty that year line up in front of a tepee facing east. "There should be nothing to block or obstruct the sun from shining on the entrance and upon the maidens to be blessed," Evelyn Breuninger, a member of the Mescalero Apache Tribal Council, has written in an official explanation of the ceremonies. "The young maidens, as they kneel, are dressed in their traditional, hand-tanned buckskin costumes. . . . Their long, black hair is left draped over their shoulders completed with two Eagle plumes attached to the back. . . . All of the motions and actions have direct meaning toward instilling good luck and health throughout the lives of the girls. Upon completion of the sacred ties, members of the family toss gifts of candy, gum, tobacco, money, and other goodies to the crowd. Years ago, the baskets of treasures were poured over the heads of the maidens." Each evening after the sun goes down, the chants of the medicine men herald the ritual dance of the maidens and dance of the mountain gods.

The uniqueness of this Apache country is apparent in the landscape. The pine forests and mountain peaks, four of which are holy to the Indians, abruptly trail off into flatlands and desert, where the wind sleeps late and awakens with a fury. This terrain has a way of attracting the sportsman. To the Inn of the Mountain Gods comes a parade of hard-core outdoorsmen eager to ride through the forests of ponderosa pine, play early-morning tennis, or fish for rainbow trout. Skiers head for nearby Sierra Blanca (considered one of the finest ski areas in the Southwest). The golfer sometimes experiences a very special kinship with nature at the inn. One player was chased in his cart by an elk. Another looked up to find a mountain lion standing somberly in the distance, eyeing him as he lined up his shot. A few astonished golfers have watched, open-mouthed, as bald eagles with 82-inch wing spans flew low over the green.

For the big-game hunter, an unforgettable experience is the annual Inn of the Mountain Gods bull elk hunt (a five-day package that includes lodgings at the inn, an Apache guide, a license, and processing of the kill, costs at least $4,695 per hunter). Because native elk have been extinct in the area since about 1900, the Tribal Council agreed in 1967 to stock the reservation. Ardent conservationists, the Apache carefully monitor the number of bull and cow elk killed. The Indian guides, believing in the philosophy of dust to dust, bury the stomach and intestines of the slaughtered elk before bringing the animal back to the inn for processing. The meat is later shipped to the hunter COD. The head, if the hunter so desires, is sent to a Dallas taxidermist for mounting. The coordinator of all this is Jo Kazhe, blonde, female, and unable to kill a fly. "They're amazed to find a woman running this," says Mrs. Kazhe, a former legal secretary from Illinois who is now married to Pete Kazhe, the first Apache to be commissioned by the U.S. Army.

Apache dancers perform at a powwow at the inn.

Inn of the Mountain Gods

The challenges of elk hunting, of course, are not for everyone. Many of the guests at the inn are prosperous Texas and Oklahoma oilmen and cattle ranchers who come with their families to relax in the cool mountain air. Dapper in fancy cowboy boots (alligator, boa constrictor, and eel skin are popular) and string ties adorned with turquoise, they unwind around the fireplace late into the evening. "Well, old John. How's your herd doing?" one Texas rancher asks a friend. In another corner, their wives, casual in well-cut jeans, discuss a Dallas charity ball and the jewelry in Rita Chino's shop.

Occasionally the conversation drifts to the Indians. Visitors at the inn cannot help but be intrigued by the customs of their hosts. Some even drive through the reservation, home to about 2,000 Apache. This is a prosperous community where the surburban-looking stone-and-wood ranch houses are equipped with all the modern conveniences, from color television sets to two-car garages. The reservation has its own general store, garage, hospital, school, five churches, swimming pool, and gymnasium. At the museum, a great granddaughter of Cochise helps compile an Apache dictionary. A granddaughter of Geronimo runs the Head Start program.

The age-old rituals persist, however, often in secret ceremonies unknown to any white man. Though most Mescalero Apache *do* go to doctors, many seek out medicine men like Melford Yuzas at crucial times in their lives. "I don't perform witchcraft," he cautions. "*I'm* not doing anything. Our creator is. I'm just the go-between." Melford is understandably closemouthed about his therapy, revealing only that he uses traditional brews of roots and herbs administered with the help of prayers and chants. Riders on his bus, hearing that he is a real Apache medicine man, pester him for cures. "What do you say, Melford?" asks a rancher from Odessa, Texas. "Can you use that magic of yours to get rid of my rheumatism?" "You're not an Indian," replies Melford. "It just won't work on you."

On the Premises: This Apache-owned resort has 240 rooms and 10 suites. The major attractions are the extraordinary mountain scenery and full range of recreational facilities. The inn has an 18-hole championship Ted Robinson golf course with a resident PGA pro; 6 outdoor tennis courts and 2 indoor ones; daily trail rides; fishing for trout in Lake Mescalero; sailing, canoeing, and swimming; skeet and trapshooting; hunting for elk, antelope, bear, and whitetail deer; skiing, from Thanksgiving through Easter; volleyball; badminton; and bicycling.

Rooms: The colors are reds and golds, like an Indian blanket. A few pottery lamps and paintings of tribal scenes add to the effect. Mostly, however, the rooms are functional and modern, not particularly atmospheric. They are generally spacious, especially the one-bedroom suites, and have nice views over the lake.

Meals: The inn's main dining room is open for breakfast, lunch, and dinner. Breakfasts, hardy and basic, are followed by fairly eclectic lunches, which feature everything from Texas chicken-fried steak to New York hot pastrami. On the dinner menu are classic entrees like prime ribs, poached salmon with dill, and trout topped with crab.

Getting There: The inn is about 130 miles from El Paso, Texas. Go north on Highway 54 from El Paso to Tularosa and take Highway 70 to Ruidoso. The inn is 3½ miles south of Ruidoso and 12 miles north of Mescalero. It is 190 miles south of Albuquerque, New Mexico. The nearest commercial airport is 42 miles away in Alamagordo, New Mexico, where the world's first atomic bomb was exploded. Airways of New Mexico flies small one- and two-engine planes into Alamagordo from Albuquerque and El Paso. A slightly larger airport, with bigger aircraft, is 70 miles away in Roswell, New Mexico. Pickup service is available.

Money Matters: Rooms at the inn are strictly on the European plan. Doubles in the high season (May 1 to October 31) run about $95, with off-season rates slightly less. Special ski, golf, and tennis packages are offered as well. The inn accepts MasterCard, Visa, American Express, Carte Blanche, and Diners Club.

Side Trips: At Ruidoso Downs, a few miles from the inn, the betting man (or interested spectator) will find a busy horse-racing season from May to September. The climactic event, billed as "the world's richest horse race," is the All-American Futurity on Labor Day, with a purse significantly larger than the Kentucky Derby. For a quieter pursuit, drive through the scenic canyons and forests and visit the Apache reservation and museum. Farther afield, White Sands National Monument is 60 miles west and the Carlsbad Caverns are 166 miles east of the inn.

Observations: The setting, sports facilities, and proximity to Indian life and culture make Inn of the Mountain Gods a unique resort. Keep in mind that the inn is in a remote corner of New Mexico. As of this writing, it does not offer top-level gourmet cuisine or accommodations but is trying hard to do so. Come for a low-key relaxing time in a beautiful spot.

Sante Fe

As the wagons went forward and the sun sunk lower, a sweep of red carnelian-coloured hills lying at the foot of the mountains came into view; they curved like two arms about a depression in the plains; and on that depression was Santa Fe at last! A thin, wavering adobe town . . . a green plaza . . . at one end a church with two earthen towers that rose high above the flatness.

The prairie town Willa Cather immortalized in her novel *Death Comes for the Archbishop* wavers no more. It bustles. Around the quaint, lamp-lined plaza where wagon trains once rumbled to a stop at the end of the Santa Fe Trail, gringos from New York and California cruise about in their BMWs and Mercedeses. The old dun-colored adobes are now boutiques and galleries selling the local turquoise and silver, often at Bloomingdale's prices. In the courtyards and patios, where Spanish doyennes once strolled with fans, the aromas of quiches and burritos waft from ever-proliferating restaurants.

Santa Fe, the timeless New Mexico city 7,000 feet up, is suddenly chic. Refugees from Hollywood and the banks of the Hudson are irrevocably hooked on the subtle charm of this small (population 48,900), dusty town that sits in the midst of vast desert. There is something, they say, about the weathered buttes and mesas in the distance, about the mountains studded with scrubby piñon trees, that affects the spirit. The sage-scented air, the painfully blue sky, even the dust balls that kick up on a windy afternoon mesmerize.

The town itself is as much an acquired taste as its tongue-searing cuisine. At first glance, everything is low, flat-topped, and mud-hued. In the heart of Santa Fe, no structure may be taller than the roof of the hotel La Fonda, which rises in tiered pueblo style at one corner of the Plaza. The one- and two-story adobes, some with balconies and tile work, stretch up and down the streets and off into the hills. The Romanesque St. Francis Cathedral just behind the Plaza to the northeast contrasts with the Palace of the Governors, a hulking block-long adobe structure that flanks the Plaza on the north. Despite its imposing name, the palace is a simple, sturdy building with carved wooden pillars and log ceiling beams (called *vigas* in these parts). Across from the palace is the buckskin-colored facade of Woolworths, one of the few old businesses around the Plaza that has not been replaced by a silver shop or gallery. The locals will tell you that when Woolworths goes, so goes old-fashioned Santa Fe.

Despite the inroads of chic, Santa Fe still has the soul of a Western town. Behind the shiny new boutiques, the hot-tub emporiums (a recent fad), and the pink and purple adobes that are springing up, a frontier ethos persists. Some of those cowboys stomping through the streets in high-heeled boots and bandanas are ersatz, all right. But a few are real. Many of those Indians selling handmade jewelry, pottery, and blueberry jam on blankets under the portal of the Palace of the Governors are direct descendants of the early Pueblo Indians, who have been in this arid country for centuries. As for those smiling cooks slinging tortillas in the adobe cafes, a few learned how from the instructions on the back of the cornmeal package. But others are using recipes handed down from their grandmothers and great grandmothers.

The City Different, as Santa Fe is called for no consistently explained reason, is a cross-cultural place. A little more than half the population claims Spanish heritage. (A number of proud families are direct descendants of the sixteenth-century colonizers.) Far fewer, around 2 percent of the people, are Indians. The rest are lumped together as Anglos, a major force in the political and commercial structure of Santa Fe. There are some who gripe that the Anglos are opening too many fast-food chains on the outskirts of town, and real-estate and brokerage firms within the city proper. For the most part, however, the three cultures mix harmoniously, at least on the surface. It is especially apparent on festival days, when everybody joins together to dance to mariachi bands, munch enchiladas, and celebrate their city's heritage.

If one is to visit Santa Fe, the most colorful time is summer or early fall. Then, the city offers not only fiestas, but Indian markets, rodeos, and a cultural platter that is almost too full. Thanks to the famed Santa Fe Opera and Chamber Music Festival, the city has been nicknamed the Salzburg of the Southwest. Its burgeoning Festival Theatre is attracting a strong repertory company and a sprinkling of Broadway stars. Santa Fe's obsession with the arts has nurtured fine museums and more galleries than may be found in any U.S. city of its size. Everything from bronze stagecoaches to Indian sand paintings can be picked up for a price. The artists themselves (many of whom can't seem to stop turning out canvases of Santa Fe's brooding Sangre de Cristo Mountains) are constantly feted at openings and exhibits.

It is, as John Crosby, founder and director of the Santa Fe Opera, once observed, "a remarkable town." Whether one's goal is partying, shopping, gallery hopping, or exploring the nearby pueblos, the journey to Santa Fe is unforgettable. Finding a place to stay is easy. But finding the right one, where the creature comforts are satisfactory and the ambience befits the landscape, is less so. However, Santa Fe has two unique and atmospheric guest ranches that are sagebrush serendipities. Each is a very special oasis in the desert.

The Bishop's Lodge

Santa Fe, New Mexico

One day about a century ago, Archbishop Lamy, a powerful French prelate sent to the New Mexican wilderness, was wandering through the foothills of the Sangre de Cristo Mountains. He came upon an apricot tree, gnarled and old but yielding especially succulent fruit. This fertile valley, decided the archbishop, would be his future retirement spot, a retreat for reflection over a life spent serving the church. A few years later, not far from the apricot tree, he built himself a small private chapel with a peaked shingle roof and a tall white steeple. With each passing season he planted new trees — cherries, apples, quinces, pears, and more apricots — until he had orchards admired all over the countryside.

Today many of the trees, including the original apricot, still stand on the grounds of The Bishop's Lodge, which grew up around the old chapel. The spirit of the archbishop also lives in the writing of Willa Cather, who fictionalized him as Father Latour in her novel *Death Comes for the Archbishop*. To the owners of this historic site, the memories of both the priest and the author are understandably revered. The hillside chapel, though available for weddings, is preserved as a sanctuary. As for Willa Cather, copies of her novel come with the territory and are sold at a brisk clip at the front desk.

Though a living memorial, The Bishop's Lodge is anything but somber. In the spring and summer, the sandy-beige stucco main lodge and four outer buildings are surrounded by gardens of roses, delphinium, verbena, and sweet peas. The swimming pool is a patch of brilliant turquoise. Over by the corral, a wrangler's chili red bandana is a moving beacon in the swirl of dust. Nearby, a few aspiring wranglers — little boys wearing newly acquired Stetsons, boots, and red plaid shirts — stare longingly at the horses from a perch near the stocked trout pond.

At the main lodge, the old confessional from the archbishop's chapel near the entrance sets the mood. This is a place where the history and heritage of the area are on display. A carving of a Franciscan monk is above the fireplace in the lobby, and a pen-and-ink drawing of a cowpoke on a dappled horse is on the wall nearby. An old New Mexican wood carving of an ox pulling a wagon rests on a table; a Navajo rug in the famous "Two Gray Hill" pattern is on the wall. Wrought-iron chandeliers dangle above rustic leather chairs and sofas with rawhide strips. A plate by the late Maria Martinez, New Mexico's most celebrated potter, is one of the most prized objects in the room. Then there is Pepé, in a category by himself. Pepé is a wooden Indian with sawed-off fingers and a straw hat who habitually sits on a chair near the front desk. Pepé, a fixture at

103

Inside the old chapel.

the resort for years, is mysteriously transported every now and then to the bed of an unsuspecting female guest. Generally, Pepé travels during the off-seasons in spring and fall, when the lodge opens its doors to small business groups, some of which have a penchant for pranks.

Summertime is when Pepé behaves, and when the lodge is at its best. This is family time. Guests from Texas and Oklahoma (approximately 55 percent of the clientele), Colorado, California, Illinois, New York, and other states come for the desert sun and the vistas across the piñon-studded mountains. Wearing shiny new boots and Ralph Lauren Western wear, they get up for early-morning breakfast rides. They return a little sore but championing the virtues of steak and eggs cooked over an open fire. Later, they paddle in the pool or try the tennis courts, where they learn that the 7,200-foot altitude takes some getting used to. Other guests saddle up their rented cars and head off into the hills to visit the pueblos or the small Spanish villages on the road to Taos.

Over the years the lodge has acquired a loyal cadre of returning fans. One of the earliest admirers was John D. Rockefeller, Sr., who wrote a letter thanking the owners for his pleasant stay in 1922. In those days, the lodge provided cars and filled them with oil. Rockefeller noted in his letter that he had been billed for more than he had needed, and could he please have a rebate. Another admirer was Walt Disney, who spent six weeks at the lodge in 1960 and played with the kids on the front porch. Musicians Erich Leinsdorf and Andre Kostelanetz also came to stay.

When a call came from the Monegasque consul in 1976 requesting quarters for Prince Rainier, the late Princess Grace, and their two daughters, the owner, Jim Thorpe, had no room at the inn. Rather than bump his regulars, he simply said no. "I offered to swap houses," he jokes. "But they didn't want to."

The Bishop's Lodge has been in the Thorpe family since 1918. Before that, the archbishop's retreat had belonged to the Pulitzer family. Newspaperman Joseph Pulitzer had purchased it for his two daughters, who constructed adobe homes not far from the hillside chapel. When they decided to sell the property,

The Bishop's Lodge

word filtered down to James R. Thorpe, a Denver mining man interested in the resort business. Thorpe snapped up the adobe buildings and 160 acres for $40,000. He soon converted the property into a guest ranch. A Denver man at heart, he spent most of his time in Colorado and hired resident managers for the lodge.

After his death in 1928, Thorpe's widow, Kathryn, moved to Santa Fe and took over the task of running the resort. In 1955, when the job got too exhausting for Mrs. Thorpe, her son, James Jr., an engineer by training, returned to Santa Fe from California. "I felt like I had pulled on an old familiar boot," he remembers.

Since then, practically the whole family has dug in their heels. Jim's wife, Lore, works closely at his side. At the stables, Jim's son, James R. Thorpe III, shares the job of corral boss with his wife, Carol. "You have a great sense of purpose, pride, and accomplishment doing this," says young Thorpe, a Swarthmore graduate who reveals his love of literature in the names he gives his horses. The stable of 65 or so includes Dante, Homer, Falstaff, and Cervantes. To the guests eager to saddle up and hit the trails, speed is often more important than names. "Are we going to get to run 'em?" asks a New York banker. "New Yorkers tend to think of a horse as if it were a machine, like a motorcycle," sighs Jimmy. A few of the Texans, he adds, regard horses as just

The dining room with an Indian mural.

another status symbol. "They brag about how they can handle their stallions and thoroughbreds. Then it turns out that it's really the *trainer* who rides them."

Of all the little white lies around the stables, perhaps the biggest number can be found on the daily sign-up sheets for trail rides. Guests are asked to jot down their riding experience, height, age, and, worst of all, weight. "We're aware of a fudge factor," reports Thorpe.

While the horsemen are out on the trails, the chef prepares for their return. Swiss-born Alfred Fahndrich, who has worked at the King David Hotel in Jerusalem, the Château Frontenac in Quebec City, the Dorado Beach in Puerto Rico, and The Arizona Biltmore in Phoenix, feels he has finally put down his roots in Santa Fe. The chef's varied culinary background is apparent in the international hodgepodge of dishes he serves up at The Bishop's Lodge: Mexican enchiladas, French quiches, Swiss veal and spaetzle, Italian scallopini, and Western barbecue. The guests sample his cuisine in a dramatic Southwestern-style dining room, where Navajo blankets and murals of Indians adorn the walls, and exposed piñon beams (*vigas*) stretch across the ceiling.

After dinner in this pretty salon, many guests retire to the El Charro Bar for a few margaritas. This dusky macho preserve is furnished with rustic leather chairs, a big copper fireplace, and an old trick saddle hanging on the wall. The saddle once belonged to Gene England, an adventurous wrangler who left the lodge to fight in a revolution in Honduras and later made a fortune ranching in Mexico. In his old age, he began returning to The Bishop's Lodge as a guest. "He'd bring me things—Indian blankets, silver, spurs," recalls Jim Thorpe, Jr. "One day he asked me if he could hang his old saddle here. The last year of his life, he gave me his hat. When a cowboy gives you his hat, that's the end." Like Archbishop Lamy, the tired old cowboy seemed to know that there is something timeless about the setting of The Bishop's Lodge.

PO Box 2367
Santa Fe, New Mexico   87501

Telephone
505-983-6377

On the Premises: Rustic yet sophisticated, The Bishop's Lodge is several rungs higher than a dude ranch. This guest ranch offers five hard-surface tennis courts, a swimming pool with adjacent whirlpool bath, hiking, golf privileges at a nearby club, and a large stable. Fishing and skeet and trapshooting are also available. In the busy summer season, the lodge arranges weekly steak fries on a terrace overlooking the mountains and brings in a mariachi band. Also in summer, the lodge offers a complimentary children's program; a staff of six counselors keeps kids busy with nature hikes, scavenger hunts, swimming, and pony rides. At mealtime, children can eat with their counselors in a separate dining room.

Rooms: The management strives for authenticity, especially in the older lodges dating back to the era of the Pulitzers. These accommodations, though small, are charmingly furnished with hand-painted Mexican pine chests, hammered silver mirrors, and draperies patterned with Navajo symbols. If you want a larger, more modern room, ask for one in Sunset, the newest lodge. A stack of piñon wood is outside your door. Inside, though the furnishings are standard, there are nice Southwestern touches in the adobe fireplace and the exposed *vigas*. In nearly every room, a fruit basket and a view across the mountains awaits.

Meals: Breakfast at the lodge is a lavish buffet of fresh fruits, cereals, homemade biscuits, muffins and Danish; at a special omelet bar, many varieties of the dish are cooked to order. The luncheon buffet is a spread of cold salads, vegetable molds, iced crab and

107

shrimp, as well as hot dishes such as chili rellenos (green chili peppers stuffed with cheddar cheese) or beef stew; the desserts are an array of tarts, cakes, meringue concoctions, and petits fours. The evening meal is served a la carte or table d'hôte, and includes classic Continental dishes.

Getting There: The Bishop's Lodge is about 3 miles north of Santa Fe. Take Interstate 25 north to the St. Francis exit in Santa Fe and stay on St. Francis to Camino Encantado, which dead-ends at Bishop's Lodge Road. Go north on Bishop's Lodge Road 1 mile and look for a sign on the right. The nearest airport is Albuquerque, about one and a half hours away. The lodge will pick up on request; a public "shuttlejack" service is available from the airport to downtown Santa Fe.

Money Matters: The resort operates on the European plan in March, April, and May, and from September 6 to the end of October, with the price of a double ranging from $78 to $115. Otherwise, a full American plan is in effect. In June the price is $145 to $190 per double room; from July 1 to September 5 the price is about $165 to $212 per double room. Credit cards are not accepted.

Side Trips: Spend a few days, even weeks, exploring the shops, galleries, and historical sites of Santa Fe. The Plaza itself, where spirited Spaniards once staged cock fights, is now the central meeting place. A little farther afield, but within walking distance, is Canyon Road, a long street lined with galleries and crafts shops. Santa Fe also has fascinating museums, including the Palace of the

Governors, which houses historical exhibits of the Museum of Santa Fe, the Wheelwright Museum of the American Indian, and the Museum of International Folk Art.

Observations: There is a very special beauty to this place that grows on the visitor. When the flowers are not in bloom, The Bishop's Lodge appears weathered and monochromatic, like the sands of Santa Fe. Come expecting a unique desert vacation; plan to be warmly welcomed and well cared for, but not excessively coddled. As the owner himself says: "Some of the jet-setters want egg foo yung at 2 A.M. They get a fast answer: no."

108

The Bishop's Lodge

15 *Rancho Encantado*

Santa Fe, New Mexico

A dusty road meanders through the parched brown hills to a cluster of parched brown adobe buildings. Cedar trees rustle in the center of a circular driveway. Outside the front door, a string (*ristra*) of red chilies dries in the mountain air. Just inside is a statue of Saint Francis carved from a cottonwood tree. They call this the "Enchanted Ranch," but they never spell out why. Yet there is something alluring about its secluded setting, its unpretentious exterior, and its authentic New Mexican ambience. No sooner had the ranch opened in 1968, than the rich, the famous, and the world-weary began flocking to its doors.

One of the earliest visitors to this resort in the high chaparral country north of Santa Fe was Maria Callas, who requested a suite. "We didn't have them yet," recalls the owner, Mrs. Betty Egan. "So we created one for her. She came and stayed a week and we expected a terrible temper." Callas, however, strolled about good-humoredly in Levi's, her dark hair hanging loose. One night, when two local men were celebrating their birthday in the dining room, she even sang happy birthday. The next year, during the filming of the Western *Cheyenne Social Club*, the cast—including Jimmy Stewart, Shirley Jones, and Henry Fonda—bunked down at Rancho Encantado. Their six-week stay coincided with the ranch's first anniversary party, a gala affair to which practically all of Santa Fe was invited. As the townsfolk milled about sipping their Coors and margaritas, they looked up in amazement to see the *Cheyenne Social Club* cast marching through their midst singing happy anniversary.

Over the years, Johnny Cash, Nelson Rockefeller, Kirk Douglas, Candice Bergen, and Sissy Spacek have all marveled at the views across the Jemez Mountains and sniffed the sage in the air. Prince Rainier, who visited Rancho Encantado with the late Princess Grace and their two daughters in 1976 (after they couldn't get rooms at The Bishop's Lodge), had an especially high-spirited time. Told by Mrs. Egan that a chair in the bar was hers, and that no one else could sit in it, the prince sneaked over in the middle of the night. The next morning Mrs. Egan found a little note on the chair: "Rainier sat here." So there was no mistake, he even stamped the paper with his royal symbol.

By now, Mrs. Egan and her family have grown accustomed to the parade of celebrities. They routinely stock the fridge in Robert Redford's room with Coors. At mealtimes, they calmly sneak him into a hidden balcony above the three-tiered dining room. Designer Ralph Lauren, too, finds his special needs well cared for at the ranch. On his first visit, Lauren wanted to rough it for a night and go camping. His wife, Ricki, however, was a bit squeamish. Hence,

Rancho Encantado

Mrs. Egan offered the use of her motor home. The Laurens gratefully accepted. They then camped out a mile or so from the ranch and soon found themselves serenaded by Mrs. Egan's nephew, Joe, who mischievously howled outside their window. On their next visit, they graduated to tents.

For the designer, the experience was both an adventure and an inspiration. Out of his desert sojourn grew his Santa Fe Collections. "Santa Fe touched something inside of me, the way the light plays on the sand," he reflects. "The colors and feel of my collections are what I saw in my head." Rancho Encantado, too, has struck a chord in Lauren. "It's homey, which is a hard commodity to find in a resort," he says. "The place has a nice privacy, too, and the setting is beautiful. It's up there in the hills and big and open and vast. There is a beautiful feeling of being a part of the sands of Santa Fe."

Ordinary folk, too, are touched by the beauty of the area and the sophisticated rusticity of the ranch. If Robert Redford can pick up his breakfast on a tray (there is no room service) and hang his clothes on wire hangers (wooden ones have so far been considered against the grain of the place), they can too. Guests especially like the loving care the management has put into the selection of New Mexican furnishings, as well as the chance to swim, ride, play tennis, even golf in the middle of the desert. From the pool, the vistas across the mountains (snow capped until late spring) are alone worth the trip.

It was the endless vistas and changelessness of the ranch that also attracted the Egans. They came, like pioneers, seeking a new life. Betty Egan, widowed in 1964, was determined to leave the family's home on Cleveland's West Side. "I decided we needed something to keep the family going, and suburban life wasn't it," she says. Hence, with her four teenage children in tow, she began an

odyssey across the Southwest, looking for that intangible something. "We were knocked out by the country," she recalls. "I decided to move to Santa Fe not long after we saw it. But what would I do? I got a notion that I could run a dude ranch. I knew nothing about running a hotel, but I knew that I liked nice things in a room and quality service."

One day, Slim Green, a saddle maker in the Santa Fe area, told Mrs. Egan about a run-down old guest ranch, Rancho del Monte. The minute she saw the crumbling, overgrown main lodge, Betty Egan said to herself: "This feels right." A few days later, the adventurous widow of a Cleveland manufacturer was the new owner of a dilapidated pile of adobe in the desert.

With true pioneer spirit, Mrs. Egan threw herself into months of renovation and remodeling. A neophyte at virtually every aspect of the hotel business, she drove her jeep into town to purchase supplies for the restaurant. After a number of trips to the local grocery, the curious proprietor finally asked just what she was doing with all this grub. When Betty told him, he gently suggested that she try a wholesale supplier, like every other restaurant.

To furnish her ranch, Mrs. Egan *did* hire a pro, a local decorator named Donald Murphy. With his help, she began turning the guest rooms into unique Southwestern hideaways. Each has its own individual touches, including Indian rugs, hammered-tin Mexican mirrors, decorative corn husk crosses ("We wanted to pay heed to the religiosity of the area," says Mrs. Egan) and authentic Mexican *equipale* chairs with pigskin seats and wicker-weave bases. The

113

baths, some of which have skylights, are decorated with whimsical, hand-painted Mexican tiles.

The main lodge at the ranch is a treasure trove of Spanish, Mexican, and colonial New Mexican arts and crafts. A pair of pope's chairs, copied from those in the Vatican, stand imposingly against one wall. Against another is an old grain chest said to have been transported to the New World with Christopher Columbus. Quarry tile flooring, rawhide tables and chairs, and a cowbell add a touch of rusticity.

At the end of the day, guests often drift into this colorful main lodge for bonhomie, margaritas, and maybe a platter of nachos (an hors d'ouevre of tostadas with melted cheese and green chili). One afternoon, in the spirit of camaraderie, a tourist from France and another from New England begin discussing the merits of the various pueblos. Soon they are joined by three more visitors. The conversation shifts to Indian jewelry and pottery and where to get it. Pretty soon, a New Yorker is divulging where to find the best enchilada in Manhattan.

Eventually, the newfound friends edge into the nearby dining room, a warm adobe salon with exposed beams and daffodils on the tables. The New York woman who had arrived in a Norma Kamali minidress has since shifted, like everyone else in the group, to jeans. The ranch imposes no dress code, and anything from Levi's and prairie skirts to tailored dresses goes. (Suits and ties are relative rarities.) But despite the informality, the menu is no chuck-wagon special. The ranch prides itself on its classic French cuisine, spiced with a few Southwestern specialties such as sour-cream chicken enchiladas and Pecos River green-chili stew (a searing concoction of tortillas, green chilies, onions, beans, and beef).

The next morning, the challenge is to work off the calories. This is often accomplished at the stables, where Ronni Egan, the eldest of Betty's kids, is the manager. The guests head briskly out for rides along the ridges and arroyos (streams, which are usually dry). "When they see the vastness of the landscape, many people feel threatened," says Cinciera, a half-Chippewa, half-French woman who is the head wrangler. "They ask: 'Are you sure you know where you're going?'" They also wonder if there are Indians out there, and are told: "Yup. In pickup trucks."

The horses themselves plod stoically along. Stoney (so named because he needs a tranquilizer every time he is wormed), Dark (a brisk walker who thinks he's an Arabian), and Duke (the head honcho), as well as the other horses in the dude string, know they've got a good thing going at Rancho Encantado. At this down-home guest ranch, where the help is treated like family and the guests like long-lost friends, the horses get Mondays off.

Route 4, Box 57C
Santa Fe, New Mexico   87501

Telephone
505-982-3537

On the Premises: This desert guest ranch has 28 rooms plus 36 nearby condominiums. The stable has a dude string of 11 horses and offers trail rides and special breakfast and steak rides. A pool and three tennis courts are on the grounds; golf can be arranged at a nearby club. The ranch's Cantina, a Western-style saloon and recreation room, is equipped with video and board games. Hunting, downhill and cross-country skiing, and nature hikes are also available.

Rooms: Each room is individually decorated with Mexican and Southwestern furniture, and bedspreads of prairie gingham or an Indian weave. In the main lodge, ask for room number 8, which has its own sun deck overlooking the mountains, a pink gingham bedspread on the king-size bed, a blue velvet settee, and a collection of nineteenth-century Texas currency in the bath. The *casitas* are slightly more spacious with two levels: downstairs is a living room with adobe fireplace and Mexican furniture; upstairs is the sleeping area with a refrigerator tucked under a shelf of hand-painted tiles; the spotless modern baths are decorated with the same colorful tiles. For a splurge, ask for a suite in Casa Piñon, a separate adobe cottage. This hideaway, often booked a year in advance, is furnished with the same eye for authenticity and detail.

Across the road from Rancho Encantado is Pueblo Encantado, a condominium community managed by the ranch. Some of the contemporary one- and two-bedroom condominiums are available for short-term rental. All of Rancho Encantado's sports and recreational facilities are available to those in the condominiums.

115

Rancho Encantado

Meals: Breakfast at the ranch is often hearty: blueberry pancakes, homemade biscuits with sausage and gravy, or perhaps huevos rancheros (two eggs, refried beans, grated cheese, and chili served on a corn tortilla). Lunch consists of sandwiches, crepes, "ranch-burgers," or maybe green-chili stew. The candlelit dinners are classically French and Continental (entrees include scallops Provençal, veal Normande, and duck à l'orange). A few Southwestern dishes add spice to the menu. The wine list is strictly domestic and even features El Viejo, a hearty red from Las Animas, New Mexico. French and Italian wines are available on request.

Getting There: Rancho Encantado is approximately 8 miles from downtown Santa Fe. Take the exit marked Tesuque off Route 285 (also known as St. Francis Drive). After the exit, follow the road for roughly 3 miles. You will find SR 22 on the right with a sign on the corner that tells you Rancho Encantado is 2 miles away. Turn right on SR 22 to the ranch. The nearest major airport is the Albuquerque, about one and a half hours away. The ranch limousine will pick up for a fee. A less expensive public "shuttlejack" service runs from the airport to downtown Santa Fe; from there, it is a 15-minute cab ride to the ranch.

Money Matters: The ranch operates on the European plan (although a modified American plan is available in November and December). Rooms at the ranch begin at $95 for a double in the main lodge and $145 for a *casita* with living room and refrigerator. Suites in Casa Piñon begin at $155. Master-Card, Visa, American Express, Carte Blanche, and Diners Club are accepted.

Side Trips: Taos, the famed artist's colony with its pueblos, galleries, and mystic mountaintop aura, is worth the 52-mile drive from the ranch. Take the so-called high road to Taos and visit the small Spanish villages along the way. Another interesting journey is to Bandelier National Monument, with its 700-year-old cave dwellings. (The monument is 35 miles from the ranch.) Closer to home are the pueblos of Santa Clara, San Ildefonso, Chimayo, and Tesuque, where you can scout for pottery and weaving and see a bit of the Indian way of life.

Observations: Virtually hidden away in the vast sands of New Mexico, Rancho Encantado is a special discovery, a luxurious and appealing retreat. Keep in mind, however, that it is small, fairly quiet, and unpretentious. This is a guest ranch, a place to bring your jeans and boots and forget about things like room service. Remember that the ranch generally closes down from after New Year's until the end of March.

16 *The Mansion on Turtle Creek*

Dallas, Texas

**The Mansion on
Turtle Creek**

I n a land of chicken-fried steak, chili cook-offs, high-heeled eel-skin cowboy boots, and a dance called the Cotton-Eyed Joe, Dallas, some argue, should consider seceding. This sophisticated city is a Texas anomaly, an enclave where boots and Stetsons are passé in the right circles. Dress is Eastern in Dallas, and culture is taken seriously. There are said to be 2,100 millionaires in Dallas County, many of whom have traveled widely abroad and returned home from the Continent they call "Yurp" with a sharpened sensitivity for high style and salon society.

Naturally, Lone Star State loners such as these need a place where they can show off their outfits from Paris and Seventh Avenue. They need a setting appropriately elegant, antique-filled, and more European than American—let alone Texan. They need The Mansion on Turtle Creek, a tastefully opulent hotel that murmurs money in a well-modulated voice.

That this is a world of dulcet digits is apparent the moment a guest noses his Mercedes, Rolls-Royce, or Jaguar into the circular driveway. On his left, he sees a terra-cotta-hued mansion built in the Mediterranean style with red tiled roof. A minaret the clear blue of the swimming pools in nearby Highland Park, Dallas's most exclusive section, rises to the sky from its roof. Slightly to the right is an enclosed promenade with arched French windows. This joins the mansion to a modern, nine-story hotel. Like the mansion, the hotel is a custom-colored salmon, a splash of pumpkin against the sky.

The choice of color is no caprice. The woman behind The Mansion on Turtle Creek is Caroline Hunt Schoellkopf, daughter of oilman H. L. Hunt, mother of five, grandmother of eight, and the author of a cookbook called *The Compleat Pumpkin Eater* (440 ways to prepare pumpkin). Mrs. Schoellkopf's passion for pumpkins began years ago. A frugal sort, she saved her children's Halloween jack-o'-lanterns and looked for ways to cook them. Naturally, when this inventive mother entered the hotel business a few years ago, she could not forget her devotion to pumpkins. In the interior of her hotel, the hallways are painted the same bleached orange as the exterior. On the menu is a savory pumpkin cheesecake, as well as a cold pumpkin soufflé drenched with liqueur. One rumor floating through the pumpkin halls is that Mrs. Schoellkopf wanted pumpkin jam placed on room-service breakfast trays, but was thwarted. "They don't do everything I suggest," she admits.

"They" is Rosewood Hotels, Inc., a company set up by Mrs. Schoellkopf and her family to own and operate The Mansion on Turtle Creek. (Rosewood's domain has since expanded to include the Remington in Houston and the Bel

Air in Los Angeles.) Rosewood began by purchasing a run-down Dallas mansion that had been built in 1925 by an Alabama-born cotton baron named Sheppard King. The cosmopolitan Mr. King had imported carved fireplaces, inlaid-wood ceilings, stained-glass windows, and wood paneling from Europe for his Dallas home. The executives of Rosewood decided to refurbish this faded glory and turn the mansion into a restaurant. (The upstairs bedrooms were converted into private meeting and dining rooms.) Then, they constructed a promenade connecting the old King estate to the modern hotel.

In furnishing the hotel, the team of decorators and designers carefully mixed old and new. A fine collection of modern art contrasts with nineteenth-century French mirrors, antique English chests, and Chinese porcelains. The man in charge of all these massive renovations and design plans was Robert D. Zimmer, a hotel interior designer who had been persuaded to move from California to Dallas to become Rosewood's first president.

Since The Mansion on Turtle Creek opened in 1981, it has aspired to be a friendly estate, not a cold hotel. The valets and front-desk personnel wear pin-striped suits by Ralph Lauren. "We're anti-uniform. We want people to feel they are arriving at a private home," explains the hotel's general manager, Alexander de Toth. The management was especially concerned that women feel at home. Each of the guest rooms was designed with a wife of a chairman of the board in mind: What would she want in her room if she were staying in on a rainy day? Hence, the hypothetical executive's wife finds herself in a generously proportioned room (averaging about 450 square feet) decorated in sophisticated taupes, golds, and peaches. At least three telephones are at her fingertips, along with a stereo and color television (discreetly concealed in a burnished armoire). A stack of upscale magazines, such as *Architectural Digest, Fortune,* and *The New Yorker*, are there for reading in bed. The sheets, of course, are white and 100 percent cotton. The bouquets of flowers are freshened frequently, and the abundant plants and trees are monitored by plant doctors. Naturally, the solid-brass fixtures in the bath are polished daily. The wicker tray by the tub is never without thick terry towels, Crabtree & Evelyn shampoo, and Hermès almond-honey soap.

Selecting each of these special touches required a meeting of summitlike magnitude. "I can remember a whole morning devoted to choosing faucets," sighs Mrs. Schoellkopf, who was closely involved in nearly every aspect of the hotel. The loving care she and her staff put into The Mansion on Turtle Creek is certainly appreciated by the guests. But another big draw of the hotel is having all the best eyes of Texas upon you in the lobby and dining rooms. Since the restaurant opened in 1980, a year before the hotel, The Mansion on Turtle Creek has become the hangout of Dallas society, Texas oil money, and world royalty, crowned or not.

Long before these guests arrive, the hotel's phones crackle with requests to be met at the airport by limousines filled with roses and to have their rooms stocked with Dom Perignon and beluga caviar. A few of the more daring ask to be met by the Texas Taxi, an independent Dallas concern that dispatches convertibles and Rolls-Royces with longhorns on the hood and tape decks that play "The Eyes of Texas Are Upon You."

No matter what their mode of transport, guests at the hotel arrive heavily laden with the latest in finery. None of those string ties or Levi's for these gentlemen. Although one regular is fond of matching his ties and massive rings (green tie, emerald ring; red tie, ruby ring), most men at The Mansion on Turtle Creek wear understated jewelry and suits from Brooks Brothers. Their ladies seem to favor Adolfo, Bill Blass, Albert Nippon, and Galanos, well accessorized with gold and diamonds. When the winter winds get brisk in Dallas, and they do, out come the sables and lynx.

The hotel is the special preserve of the Dallas dynasties: Hunts, Strausses, Murchisons (Clint Jr. owns the Dallas Cowboys), and Coxes. They frequent it for lunch, dinner, and private parties. "It's a first-rate place to go," says Robert Strauss, former chairman of the Democratic National Committee. His sister-in-law Annette Strauss, a woman prominent in Dallas arts and society, adds: "I feel like I'm at home when I go there." The city's adopted Dynasty—the cast of TV's "Dallas"—also checks into the hotel on a regular basis. "I think it's one of the best hotels in America," says J. R. Ewing, sometimes known as Larry Hagman. "The ambience is great. You go in and there are 600 tulips and daisies or something when you enter. They go out of their way to make you feel special. So few hotels give a damn anymore." Fellow actor James Garner and singer Tony Bennett might have wished the hotel gave a little less of a damn about dress codes. Both were refused entrance to the restaurant because they lacked ties. Burt Reynolds borrowed one from a staffer and promptly spilled a little tortilla soup on it.

When the queen of Thailand came to town, it was she who set a few standards. Well in advance of Queen Sirikit's stay at The Mansion on Turtle Creek in 1981, a memo went out to staffers outlining methods of address ("Your Majesty"), matters of protocol (never show royalty the soles of your shoes), and unacceptable topics (*The King and I*, politics, and Buddha). Her Majesty, who arrived with 250 pieces of Louis Vuitton luggage and took 40 rooms on two floors, wanted tea one evening. The kettle in her rooms wouldn't do, so a call was made to a Neiman-Marcus executive, who opened the store after hours so that the proper teapot could be acquired.

Even for nonroyalty, the staff is used to catering to every request. A personal shopper can be summoned on a second's notice to show a visiting executive's wife the wonders of Neiman-Marcus. A carriage with Clydesdales can be hired for a ride along Turtle Creek, actually more a river than a creek. When Bill Cosby wanted pizza in the middle of the night, he got it, and when two Arabs craved Chinese food at 3 A.M., a bellboy drove them to a local hangout.

Most guests do their eating right in the hotel's dining rooms. The main dining area, originally the salon of the King residence, has a ceiling made of 2,400 pieces of enameled and inlaid wood. The limestone fireplace is a reproduction of one in Bromley Castle in England. Adorning the walls is a collection of nineteenth-century Spode china. To the Dallas cognoscenti, the most-coveted seats are the front banquettes and a large round table near the pastry chef's prized display. Adjacent to the main dining room is a former library that now serves as part of the restaurant. The highlight of this room is a set of stained-glass windows depicting the British barons witnessing the signing of the Magna Carta at Runnymede.

After dinner in such surroundings, many patrons drift over to the lounge and bar area, an imposing, rather masculine preserve with forest green walls and a 20-foot parquet bar. The mounted deer and antelope heads belong to Mrs. Schoellkopf's husband, Buddy. One of the hotel's decorators, the story goes, tried to select only those heads with sweet expressions.

To the clientele at the bar, smiling antelope are of little concern. Besides the hotel regulars, the crowd consists of young, upcoming Dallas business types. "They're into what we call R&I, ranching and investments," explains a hotel staffer. "They're professional Texans. They believe in living and being happy and doing well in the family business." Unlike New Yorkers, who crowd a bar like a herd of longhorn, the Dallas bunch sit solidly on stools. "Texans who know *better*," reports a local, "don't stand up at bars."

They do, however, mill about happily at parties. Many in Dallas still talk about the one to celebrate the opening of The Mansion on Turtle Creek in the spring of 1981. From Rome, New York, Chicago, Mexico, El Paso, Amarillo, and Houston they came, paying $1,000 a couple (the money went to charity) for two days of nonstop partying. A fleet of limousines was dispatched to meet the distinguished guests at the airport. The arriving crowd found their rooms filled with fresh peonies and outfitted with hand-painted bottles of Perrier-Jouet champagne (with glasses to match), a little carafe of crème de cassis to mix with the champagne, and a Neiman-Marcus credit card.

As the weekend progressed, the out-of-towners joined the local Dallas gentry for a round of cocktail parties and dinners. At one cocktail hour, a harpist played as the guests sampled four different kinds of caviar (beluga, osetra, sevruga, and North American sturgeon roe), and sipped one domestic and three French brands of champagne. That night, in black tie, the guests gathered in the restaurant for steak and salmon tartare, clams, oysters, cheese, pâté, and more caviar. Then came dinner. About this time, one partygoer turned to another and remarked that not since Edna Ferber's novel *Giant* had there been a gathering such as this in Texas. Oh, no, said her companion. That image was all wrong for today's Texas. Surely, the party was more like one Jay Gatsby would have thrown. Both agreed on another point. If a bomb were to have been dropped on The Mansion on Turtle Creek that weekend, the nation's, perhaps the world's, oil business would have become leaderless.

2821 Turtle Creek Boulevard,
Dallas, Texas   75219

Telephone
214-559-2100

On the Premises: This impeccable, small hotel is run like a private estate. It has 129 rooms, 14 suites, swimming pool, and sun deck. Tennis, polo, golf (two championship courses), squash, and raquetball are available at nearby clubs on seconds' notice.

Rooms: Virtually all accommodations look like a Bloomingdale's model room. There are muted floral draperies, classic roll-arm sofas, and French armoires. The baths, scented with fresh flowers on the makeup table, are a sea of marble, solid brass, and mirrors. If possible, splurge on a suite. Terrace Suite 919 has a canopy bed, two baths, a peach living room with a wet bar, a kitchen with microwave oven, and a garbage compactor (in case you want to give a little party), and a large, plant-filled terrace.

Meals: Breakfast is served in the Promenade, a pretty, plant-filled arcade connecting the mansion and the hotel. Many Dallas businessmen drop in here daily for the Belgian waffles, apple pancakes, eggs Benedict, homemade pumpkin muffins, and Texas-size croissants (they sometimes call in their orders from their limousines). Lunch is served in the restaurant, where one can order anything from light seafood salad to steak tartare. The weekend brunches (try the fettucine Gorgonzola, omelets, and chili) are prime times for people watching. Likewise, dinner is a chance to take in the Dallas scene. The a la carte menu is duly sophisticated: braised squab with raspberries, pheasant with wild mushrooms, pompano en papillotte, and patridge cocotte are among the choices.

Getting There: The hotel is about 30 minutes from the Dallas–Fort Worth Airport on the Stemmons Freeway. Take the Oak Lawn exit off the freeway, turn left, and go about 2 miles on Oak Lawn; then take a right on Gillespie and the entrance to the hotel is on the right. The Mansion on Turtle Creek will gladly send a Rolls-Royce, Austin Princess, or a "superstretch" limo equipped with television, bar, and video games to the airport. Any form of transportation can be filled with roses on request.

Money Matters: The hotel operates on the European plan, with doubles ranging from $170 to $195 per room, per night; suites range from $350 to $550. All major credit cards are accepted.

Side Trips: The attractions of Dallas itself, including Neiman-Marcus; countless art galleries, museums, boutiques; and the Dallas Symphony are all within a short walk or drive from the hotel. Farther afield, one can visit Southfork, J. R. Ewing's ranch.

Observations: This is a small, perfect stone in the oversize diamond necklace that is Dallas. Although it is technically a big-city American hotel, in mood and philosophy The Mansion on Turtle Creek is a European retreat for those who want to be pampered at any price. Don't come expecting a full range of resort activities. However, the best of everything can be arranged at a moment's notice. Dallas Cowboy tickets? Just dial the concierge. A selection of sables from the top furrier in town? That, too, can be easily handled.

123

17 *Deer Valley Resort*

Park City, Utah

The famed Utah powder feathers the faces of skiers traversing toward the foot of Bald Eagle Mountain. A New Yorker, eager to join their ranks, drives hurriedly up to the base lodge.

Suddenly, his outraged cries mingle with the wind. "Hey! Stop that! Thief!" he bellows as a figure in a green ski parka and hat hauls his skis from the car roof. "I'm just *unloading* them, sir," says the attendant. "It's one of the services we provide here at Deer Valley." Slightly mollified, but still disbelieving, the New Yorker offers a tip. It is politely refused. Grabbing his Rossignols, he then glances about for a place to leave them while he has breakfast. He is directed to the ski corral, literally a Western corral where skis are checked for an hour, a day, or overnight. "No, sir," he is told. "There is no charge." Once again, his tip is refused.

By this time, the New Yorker is getting increasingly agitated. Okay, so they provide a few nice free services. But wait a minute. It's Sunday. It's the height of the ski season. Why is there no line at the ticket windows? Why is there no line at the lift? Why is everyone smiling? What's *wrong* here?

Essentially, nothing. Deer Valley just happens to be run by people who want to take the masochism out of skiing. They are devoted to the principle that one can ski the American West and not feel herded like a longhorn. Even better, they believe that skiers should be pampered. "Skiers should only have to worry about who is going to care for them next," says Stein Eriksen, the Norwegian 1952 Olympic gold medalist who is Deer Valley's director of skiing. "You know, America has been *losing* the skiers who want enjoyment and amenities. They go to Europe to those little pensions that welcome you. Well, we want them back!"

Gradually, they are coming. Deer Valley opened in the 1981–82 winter season and was almost immediately proclaimed the ultimate resort by ski writers. Newcomers found that it was not merely a mountain (actually two, Bald Eagle and Bald, with a third, Flagstaff, scheduled to open in 1984–85) but a concept. As Eriksen himself explains it: "The challenges are there if you want them. But we want to please people the rest of the time, too. We have tea and pastry and backgammon for Grandma while she watches her granddaughter ski." Mama and Papa will find an assortment of condominium and hotel facilities luxuriously equipped with everything from Betamaxes to family-size hot tubs. "Ja, ja, we're exclusive," nods Eriksen. "But we're not snobbish."

The word most commonly heard around Deer Valley is *classy*. The two slopeside lodges, Snow Park and Silver Lake, look more like country clubs than places to warm up between runs. Angular, shiny cedar structures on the outside, they are paneled and polished on the inside. Brass railings and fixtures gleam in the light of the huge fireplaces made of stones from south Utah quarries. Even in the restrooms the fixtures are brass, and the sink tops are a smooth granite that looks like marble. Early on, somebody eyed these appointments, swank for the mountains, and called Deer Valley the "Mercedes of ski resorts."

One sunny, 35-degree December day, the crowd sipping drinks and tanning themselves on the deck of Silver Lake Lodge looked like a Mercedes bunch. Most wore the unofficial Deer Valley uniform, a snug-fitting, Italian-made jump suit (better than a parka and ski pants for keeping dry in the waist-high Utah powder). At one table, the wife of a Brazilian industrialist sported a rainbow-hued jump suit with matching headband. At another, a California millionaire and his wife wore matching mauve suits, hers with little puffed shoulders. "You don't see many people skiing in jeans here," noted a regular. "This is a slightly older, affluent crowd. How many people become affluent by the time they are twenty?"

Deer Valley Resort

With age and affluence, it appears, comes a recognition that the mountain doesn't have to be conquered *right now*. The Deer Valley skiers sleep late and meander over to the lifts around 10 or 11 A.M. for a few leisurely runs before lunch. Arriving at the ticket windows, they claim the reservations their secretaries made days, even weeks, before. (It is this reservation system, suggested but not required, along with a limit of 2,900 skiers on the slopes, that keeps lift lines to a maximum wait of five minutes.) On the Carpenter lift, one of six at Deer Valley, two Salt Lake City businessmen trade stock tips as they glide by a grove of aspen. Over at the Wasatch lift, which carries more-expert skiers to the top of 9,400-foot Bald Mountain, an Eastern prep-school student on vacation with her parents is breathing hard. Could it be the altitude, or the rumor she heard on the slopes that Robert Redford was just seen heading down an expert trail called Ruins of Pompeii? (Actually, Redford comes often, and finds that he is less hassled at Deer Valley than at his own ski resort, Sundance, in nearby Provo.)

For most skiers, the slopes themselves are the thrill. This is by no means the vicious, gut-numbing terrain of the Alps or even of more rugged Western resorts like Snowbird. Though Deer Valley has its share of steep, mogulled runs like Hawk Eye and Grizzly, it is noteworthy for its immaculately groomed trails. On all but the most expert trails, icy patches, ruts, and moguls are unheard of. The management likes to boast that every trail follows the natural fall line of the mountain, the path a snowball would roll if it tumbled straight down. They'll also tell you that every trail faces north or northeast, meaning that the sun isn't in your face when you ski or melting that powder into slush.

The skier, freed from the usual worries about ice or harrowing, unexpected turns, is able to luxuriate in his surroundings. The pine- and aspen-studded peaks of Utah's Wasatch Mountain Range stretch as far as the eye can see. Deep in the valley, the lights of Park City, an old mining town resurrected into a ski mecca, twinkle in the blinding light of the snow. A draft of wind and darkening clouds hint of a storm coming in across the deserts of Nevada. There is that promise of new snow and fresh powder in the air. Even Stein Eriksen, veteran of more than half a century on the slopes, is moved. "Being up here, seeing the trees and the snow and looking as far as the eye can see across the mountains, you know you were really meant to be involved with nature. You know what life is all about."

But one also has to eat, and the Deer Valley management believes in mountain gourmandizing. The man who created Deer Valley, Aspen-based businessman Edgar B. Stern, also owns San Francisco's exclusive Stanford Court Hotel. "We approached this operation of a ski area like we were establishing a fine hotel," says Stern. "We wanted people to have a peaceful, unhassled experience and good food. I remember how I hated going skiing and having bad food." The president of Deer Valley, Jim Nassikas, who is also the president of the Stanford Court, agrees. So does Jim's son, Bill Nassikas, the resort's food and beverage director. They have installed a La Varenne-trained chef and a menu that unquestionably deserves mountain laurels. Instead of the usual hot dogs on paper plates, Deer Valley offers nouvelle cuisine and Continental dishes in the Café Mariposa at Silver Lake Lodge. Over fresh salmon caught only 24 hours earlier in the waters off Stein Eriksen's Norway, Maine lobster straight from the traps, or bluepoint oysters from Chesapeake Bay, diners face a dilemma:

A condominium available through Deer Valley Lodging (*above*) and a room at the Stein Eriksen Lodge (*right*).

whether to have a dacquoise and a third cup of coffee, or return to the slopes. "I think maybe I've had enough skiing for today," observes a Mariposa patron with a Southern drawl. She signals to the waiter, then contentedly surveys the pretty, woodsy room. A carved wooden deer from Germany is on the fireplace. The Norman hutch and polished oak floors shine in the light of the brass Victorian wall lamps. A Jacobean sideboard is covered with the pastry chef's art.

A few steps away in the Snuggery, or down the mountain at the Huggery in Snow Park Lodge, dining is cafeteria style. Separate food islands crafted out of Alaskan yellow cedar and trimmed in brass are designed to keep lines to a minimum. In the dead of winter, giant strawberries, half-moons of melon, and mounds of grapes are piled high on one of the islands. At another, a chef in a white toque carves roast baron of beef and stuffed loin of pork. "I come here for the food," says a Princess Diana look-alike in skintight stretch pants. "Why go to a ski resort and eat junk when you can have this?" A five-year-old boy munching a homemade chocolate-chip cookie the size of a small Frisbee seems to agree. So does the silver-haired woman in silver fox jacket and matching gray slacks who has come for the pasta Niçoise served on fine china, and certainly *not* to ski.

In the late afternoons at Deer Valley, after the sun has disappeared below the peaks and the snowcats have been dispatched for the nightly grooming of the slopes, the action shifts. Some folks gather in one of the lounges for a drink and a rehashing of the day's runs. Others disappear into the privacy of their own condominiums. These cedar-and-brick chalets dot the Deer Valley landscape and are even clustered halfway up the mountain near Silver Lake Lodge. They are sleekly modern inside, with special touches like brass handrails, heat-sensitive light switches, solid oak kitchens, glossy custom-made lacquered chests and tables, and color cable TV. Some are on one level; others are duplex and triplex. Almost every condominium has at least one whirlpool bath and a few have private hot tubs adjacent to the living room. The management is considering supplying rubber ducks but is still deciding whether that fits their image. They do, however, provide masseurs and masseuses to soothe skiers after a rough day on the slopes. Virtually any request, including the one from the Hollywood producer who wanted a grand piano in his condomininium during his 20-day stay, is cheerfully addressed and generally fulfilled.

Another choice of accommodations at Deer Valley is the Stein Eriksen Lodge, a Scandinavian-style structure with overhanging eaves. Located at Silver Lake, this is a place where guests can go to the back door, slip into their skis (brought up from a heated locker by a bellboy) and slide a few steps to the lift. Eriksen himself displays a proprietary air not only about the proximity of the skiing, but about the solid-brass fixtures, the deer lamps, and the quilted comforters patterned in deep Norwegian reds, blues, and greens. He has even installed his 130 trophies and 50 medals in a case in the forest green lobby. A 40-foot-high tapestry depicting the major events in his life extends upward toward the vaulted ceiling. The bronze statue of a skier poised in less-than-perfect form by the fireplace is not, Stein is quick to point out, a model of himself. "I try to keep my skis together," he says.

Out on the slopes, Stein is happy to demonstrate his perfect form, if not necessarily the aerial flips that helped launch the freestyle skiing phenomenon. "So nice of you to meet me," he jokes to a visiting member of the press before focusing his attention on another skier's form. "Do you feel a little awkward doing a right turn?" he asks gently. Then, he proceeds to offer suggestions.

After a lifetime of skiing, Eriksen has gained a new perspective on what people want out of the sport. "They want to feel good and look good on skis. Most people don't want challenges jumping out at them every minute. That's why Deer Valley is so unique," he says. "I have skied places that offer longer runs and maybe more skiing. But not the full package: the services, the courtesies, and the ultimate challenge of the mountain."

🛏 🍴 🚕 💲 ❓

PO Box 889
Park City, Utah   84060

Telephone
801-649-1000 for general information
801-649-4149 for ski reservations
801-649-4040 or 800-453-3833 for
Deer Valley lodging
801-649-3700 or 800-453-1302 for the
Stein Eriksen Lodge.

130

**Deer Valley
Resort**

On the Premises: Deer Valley is part of a new, sprawling development a few minutes from downtown Park City, Utah. Two ski lodges, various clusters of condominium units, and a slopeside hotel are all integrated into the mountain landscape. The 12-year development plan calls for an entire mountain village at Silver Lake, 80 ski runs, 15 lifts, and 3 mountains in operation. Currently, Deer Valley offers skiers 6 chair lifts serving 32 runs over 2 mountains: Bald Mountain (elevation 9,400 feet) and Bald Eagle Mountain (elevation 8,400 feet). Some runs are at least a mile long, with uninterrupted descents of 1,400 feet; the majority of the runs fall into the intermediate to advanced-intermediate range. Helicopter skiing with a guide can be arranged for advanced skiers. Deer Valley also offers a ski school, rentals and storage, a ski shop, and child-care facilities (for which there is a charge).

For nonskiers at Deer Valley, there are about 25 tennis courts, 2 golf courses, and a stable in the Park City area. The Stein Eriksen Lodge has a heated, year-round pool and an exercise room.

Rooms: Skiers at Deer Valley may opt for any of the 5,000 accommodations in the Park City area, and the resort will gladly make suggestions. However, many skiers prefer the proximity of the 105 condominium units (rented on a three-night-minimum basis) by Deer Valley Lodging, or the Stein Eriksen

Lodge, a condominium hotel. The Deer Valley Lodging condos are spread out all over the property and have a whirlpool bath in almost every unit, cable color TV, microwave ovens, and garbage compactors. Each of the two- to four-bedroom units is individually decorated (most with contemporary furniture and prints) and highlighted with such whimsical accessories as procelain rabbits, wooden foxes, and painted ducks fashioned into towel racks. Others are outfitted with Crabtree & Evelyn preserves and jars of dried pasta. Towels are changed daily and linens every few days (regular maid service is available for an additional charge).

At the Stein Eriksen Lodge, the decor in the hotel rooms is country Norwegian, and very charming. Each of the 30 two- and three-bedroom suites has several Jacuzzi-type tubs outfitted with gold jets, mountain views, an outstanding kitchen with hand-painted Portuguese tiles, and telephones in every bath. There is full concierge, maid, and room service.

Meals: Skiers appreciating a big breakfast head for the Huggery at Snow Park Lodge. There they will find omelets, smoked pork chops, buckwheat pancakes with Vermont maple syrup, a natural-food buffet heaped high with granola, yogurt, and fruits, and freshly baked croissants and pastries. A cafeteria-style lunch is served in both the Huggery and the Snuggery (slopeside at Silver Lake). Deli sandwiches and hamburgers are available, but so is gourmet fare like duck à l'orange, paupiettes of Dover sole with lobster sauce, and beef Wellington. Many skiers favor the natural-food section, which at lunch is laden with salads of chicken curry, Korean cabbage, pear and yogurt, cold pasta, Chinese snow peas, dilled cucumber, and so on. A more elegant sit-down lunch or dinner is available in the Café Mariposa, where the entrees include rack of lamb al pesto, veal chops in a creamed chive sauce, and tenderloin of beef. At the Stein Eriksen Lodge, the

The deck at Snow Park Lodge.

Birkebeiner Room (named for the birch-bark leggings worn by thirteenth-century Norwegian skiers) serves breakfast, lunch, and a la carte dinners. In the more elaborate Glitretind Room (this one named for a Norwegian mountain), lunch and a five-course dinner are served.

Each accommodation at Deer Valley Lodging or the Stein Eriksen Lodge has its own kitchen, and some guests prefer to cook for themselves. The management will gladly do your shopping, and will provide everything from milk and eggs to all the fixings for a spaghetti or chili dinner. (If fresh trout or a porterhouse is what you want, no problem there, either.)

Getting There: Deer Valley is a 45-minute drive from the Salt Lake City Airport; take Interstate-80 east to the Park City exit and go 6 miles on Route 224 to Park City; turn left at the Kimball Art Center and follow the signs.

Money Matters: An all-day lift ticket for adults at Deer Valley costs $23 (half-day is $15). Condominiums at Deer Valley Lodging in the regular winter season (January 3 to April 1) range from $200 to $325 per night, per condo. At the Stein Eriksen Lodge, prices range from $80 per night for a hotel room to $525 per night for a large condo suite. Both facilities accept all major credit cards.

Side Trips: Park City, down the mountain from Deer Valley, is a picturesque little town with Victorian gingerbread houses, cowboy bars, and boutiques selling everything from Stetsons to pâté molds. For skiers there are slopes at Park City and Park West; virtually all the Utah ski resorts, including Alta, Snowbird, Brighton, Sundance, and Solitude, are within an hour's drive from Deer Valley. In Salt Lake City the major attraction is the famed Mormon Temple.

Observations: "This isn't a place for macho skiers," notes one guest, and in some measure that is true. The folks who come to Deer Valley like a heady, tough run, of course, but they also want to enjoy the good life. The mood is less gung ho than at some other resorts, and the atmosphere is more relaxed. Truly expert skiers may miss the array of precipices that hatched the killer image of a mountain like Snowbird; they may also wish the runs were longer. For most skiers, however, the combination of superbly groomed trails, excellent food and services, and almost no waiting at the lifts is a mountain experience not to be missed.

18 *The Golden Door*

Escondido, California

132

I t is 6:30 A.M., half an hour before the local rooster unruffles his feathers and crows. Through the early morning mist, a line of bodies, swaddled in sweat suits, ascends a mountain trail. Heads bowed, bodies straining, the hikers push onward to the top. As they near the final hurdle, Heartbreak Hill, they puff past avocado trees, the fruit of which (at 280 calories per small serving) is far too fattening for them to eat. At the crest of the mountain, they gaze out at the Pacific, shrouded by clouds. The soul sighs. The body rallies at the prospect of going down.

A half-hour later, the 3-mile trek over, the climbers return to their rooms at The Golden Door. Soon comes a discreet knock. Breakfast. What does today's tray have to offer? A silver pot of herbal tea. A poached egg in a fluted white cup. A tiny bowl of bran mixed, no *laced*, with raisins and nuts. But what's this in the golden wrapper? A quarter of a piece of toast, real, whole wheat, freshly baked toast. A *quarter* of a piece. "At first," sighs a middle-aged woman with great longing in her voice, "I looked at the gold paper and thought it was Almond Roca." Other Golden Door guests have been known to organize an impromptu contest to see who can get the most bites out of the tiny morsel of toast.

Losing pounds and inches clearly requires gaining resourcefulness — and maintaining good humor. The Golden Door, one of America's oldest and most respected fitness spas, has a returning coterie of converts who know how to keep chins up and weight down. They migrate year after year to this 157-acre ranch hidden in the rugged mountains outside San Diego. Even the first-timers quickly adapt to the philosophy that (eating) less is more. Naturally, they wince and moan a bit to learn that the refrigerator in the kitchen is padlocked, the cheesecake, though delicious, is made of tofu, and the cocktails are cool, wet, fruity — and nonalcoholic.

The Golden Door firmly believes that one rigorous and reflective week can, and often does, change your life. The key is moderation. This is no medieval torture chamber filled with fiendish machines. Nor is it a eucalyptus-scented sanctuary for salves and balms. Saunas and massages do exist, of course, judiciously incorporated into a regime of hikes, water exercises, and "let it burn" calisthenics.

The festivities, if they can so be called, commence on Sunday. Some women (men, too, during The Golden Door's nine annual men's weeks and seven couples' weeks) begin expiating the sins of modern life long before they arrive.

133

They religiously diet and exercise in anticipation. But others sneak in a last-minute binge. Saturday night is often the time for a hearty last supper. Or last suppers. Sunday, in the airplane or on the road, they even gobble two breakfasts. A young woman from Beverly Hills, who drove down with a friend, openly admits: "We stopped for two malteds on the way."

Arriving at The Golden Door, most people temporarily shelve thoughts of food. The surroundings breed more lofty reflections. The spa's founder, Deborah Szekely, believes an aura of serenity is as essential to dieters as calorie counting. This Brooklyn-born woman, daughter of early vegetarians (her mother was vice-president of the New York Vegetarian Society in 1926), has developed her philosophies on health and environment over many years. In 1940 she and her first husband, Edmond Szekely, opened a spa called Rancho La Puerta in Baja, California. Then, in 1958, Deborah founded The Golden Door in an adobe hacienda in Escondido. When the state announced plans to build a new highway through the property in 1975, she built a second Golden Door a mile or so away. As a longtime student of Japanese art and culture, she designed her new spa to resemble a Japanese inn.

Guests enter via a curving, 140-foot footbridge that spans a camellia-banked stream. They pull open the golden door (it does exist, made of hammered brass with a tree-of-life motif inlaid with lapis and jade). Inside the reception area, rattan sofas and chairs upholstered in a gray and green cloud pattern invite the out of shape to rest before the calorie-burning ordeal begins. On one wall is a screen depicting the exploits of Genji, a sort of Japanese Don Juan. Through the sliding shoji doors (typical of a Japanese house), visitors look out at the gray tile roofs and ochre stucco walls of the adjoining buildings. Japanese black pines stir slightly in the breeze. The gong of a Buddhist temple bell constructed in 1705 marks the hour.

The world fleetingly intervenes. Guests are welcomed and asked to please lock up their jewelry in special safe-deposit boxes. "It makes you feel a little like checking into a hospital," mutters one woman. Soon, however, she will come to understand, even appreciate, The Golden Door's no-adornment philosophy. Spending a week at the spa is a little like peeling off an old skin. Guests are asked to shed their baubles, their makeup, even their clothes. Most women wear the regulation wardrobe: beige and maroon warm-up suit, blue shorts and a T-shirt on hotter days, and flowing blue-and-white kimonos in the evening. A few guests do come to dinner in casual dresses or slacks, but, notes one woman, "the kimono is the great leveler." Observes another Golden Door devotee: "It has to do with the syndrome of camp and boarding school. They put you in uniform."

The Golden Door's director, Annharriet Buck, explains that the uniforms

have an important behavioral function at the spa. "The women are wearing none of the things that usually define them. They look in the mirror and they see their faces and their bodies. For some, it has a shock value." This, she adds, often leads to soul-searching and self-analysis as the week progresses. "People go home and they write to us that they have started a new business, altered a relationship, fired a troublesome employee, or in some way changed their life."

On their first morning, 34 women, groggy, discombobulated, and wondering, perhaps, how they got into this, assemble for a 6:15 warm-up preceeding the daily hike. Stretching and bending, saying little, they are a cross section of American womanhood. A young mother struggling to shed the weight of her last pregnancy sets off up the mountain behind the sleek, middle-aged wife of an oilman. A New York realtor trudges behind a San Francisco doctor. Two mother-and-daughter teams are in the group, along with an elderly grandmother type who later proves a whiz at water sports. This week, they are a low-key group.

The Golden Door celebrity contingent (Joanna Carson, Rhonda Fleming, Cindy Williams, Barbara Howar, Bill Blass, and Cher have all enrolled in the program) is absent. When the famous *are* in residence, they tend to behave like everybody else.

As the day progresses at The Golden Door, the guests move from class to class, pausing every few hours for juice or potassium broth and raw vegetables. Their individual schedules, prearranged by staffers, are lettered on little paper fans the women wear pinned to their warm-up suits. "We want people to eliminate all need for decision making when they are here," explains director Buck. "We like to keep it a magical experience and allow the women to sink into it."

The Golden Door

A Japanese-style garden
and walkway (*above*) and the
famous golden doors
(*left*).

The guest quarters.

The women themselves show remarkable willingness. Very few skip class or slip up to the hillside solarium for nude sunbathing. Besides, there are occasional rewards, such as a soothing facial mask of Chinese clay and camphor, a pedicure or an herbal wrap in which the body is swathed, mummylike, in layers of hot sheets boiled in rosemary and eucalyptus. Then, too, there is the daily massage, a full, hedonistic hour in the privacy of one's room. Other luxuries include individual skin analyses, makeup lessons, eyebrow arches, even lash tints. A San Diego hairstylist comes by early in the week to give consultations, and returns near the end to do any cutting or reshaping requested by guests. In between, most women succumb to having their locks coated daily with a mixture of avocado and rose oil, which serves as protection from the sun, sweat, and chlorine. "My hair feels a little yucky this way," gripes one guest. "But I don't *really* mind. I know it's good for me."

So is the low-fat, low-calorie cuisine. Resident Chef Michel Stroot is a maestro at extracting a pound of flesh (actually 3 to 5 pounds is the average weekly loss) as painlessly as possible. Stroot, a soft-spoken Belgian, prepares unexpectedly filling Japanese dishes and nouvelle cuisine, beautifully presented on The Golden Door's collection of Oriental pottery. The daily caloric intake comes to about 900 calories. Women who request 500- or 700-calorie diets get smaller portions and sometimes no dessert. Diehard dieters can even go on a liquid regime two days a week. For those who want to maintain, possibly *gain* weight, the portions and calorie counts increase to 1,100, 1,400, even higher on occasion.

To Chef Stroot, it's not so much the size of the serving that matters as the style in which it is presented. His meals, most of which are prepared with fruits and vegetables grown in The Golden Door's organic gardens (famished guests have been know to snitch strawberries), are colorful still lifes. "If the eye is pleased, you're not so aware that you are eating less," explains Stroot. Hence, he selects striking garnishes like pimento or orange nasturtium (which is edible). The chef also believes in filling the plate, even if it's only with little mounds of shredded carrots, lettuce, or bean sprouts. "You must never have an empty spot!" he insists.

Thanks to the efforts of Stroot and the rest of the staff, most women progress through the week without feeling deprived. In fact, after a midweek slump in mood, there is a noticeable euphoria. "By the end of the week, you feel so good about yourself," declares a San Clemente wife and mother. "When you get home, the mood lasts for months. My husband likes me much better after a week at The Golden Door." To other women, a stay at The Golden Door is a necessary replenishment. "For years I've been like a cornucopia, giving to my husband, my children, my parents. But what about *me*?" asks a Texan. "Here, I'm getting some of *myself* back."

138

The Golden Door

A fan-shaped hot tub in the bathhouse.

PO Box 1567
Escondido, California   92025

Telephone
714-744-5777

On the Premises: Located in a tranquil mountain setting, The Golden Door accommodates 34 women (and men during occasional men's weeks). Both sexes follow essentially the same program of calisthenics, aerobics, and water sports. In addition, there is a full beauty program. (During men's weeks, masseurs instead of masseuses do the job. The all-female beauty staff keeps the doors open in their treatment rooms when working on men.) In the spa's authentic Japanese bathhouse, the sound of a wooden

flute fills the air as guests soak in the communal, fan-shaped hot tub. The Golden Door also offers nightly lectures on topics ranging from handwriting analysis to nutrition. Each guest receives stationary with her name hand-lettered in gold, a gift certificate to the boutique, and an individual exercise tape tailored to her specific needs.

Rooms: Each guest has a private room in one of the clusters of single-story stucco buildings accentuated by overhanging Japanese eaves. The fabrics are restful blues and beiges swirled into prints and cloud patterns. The accents are Japanese: Oriental silk screens and woodcuts adorn the walls; shoji screens slide inside the jalousie windows; a wood carving of a pagoda stands in a glass case. In the baths, Western in their modernity, The Golden Door's skin products are in the cabinets. Behind each room is a private little patio called the moon-viewing deck, where guests are encouraged to contemplate the groves of palm and bamboo, the sand gardens, the trickling brooks, and the stars.

139

Meals: The lemon soufflé is made with cottage cheese; the carob mousse is eaten with a demitasse spoon to make it last longer. But fear not. The Golden Door serves innovative gourmet cuisine that makes up in taste and presentation what it lacks in calories. A different breakfast is presented each morning; the selections include cheese toast, strawberries and yogurt, and a cereal made of oats, figs, and nuts. Lunch, eaten poolside or in the dining room, is a fairly light meal consisting of fruit plates, shrimp or turkey salads, or possibly a vegetable-based quiche. The evening meal begins with a nonalcoholic cocktail of diluted juice and crudités (stuffed mushrooms, 25 calories each, are offered once during the week). Then comes soup or salad and an entree that depends on the chef's whim and what is fresh. Selections include broiled lemon swordfish, chicken yakatori, Cornish game hen with ginger dressing, and cold lobster. For dessert there might be a kiwi fruit salad, fresh strawberries, or a pear soufflé. On the last night, each guest gets a glass of wine or champagne.

Getting There: Private planes fly into nearby Palomar Airport; the closest commercial field is in San Diego, about 40 miles away. The Golden Door sends a driver to meet each guest at the airport at no extra charge. Those who prefer to drive should take Highway 78 (which connects with the San Diego Freeway and the Santa Ana Freeway) to Escondido. Take the Riverside turnoff onto Interstate 15 north and continue for 5 miles. Watch for the Deer Springs Road sign, which will be a right-hand turnoff. Continue 1 mile west to 777 Deer Springs Road. The Golden Door will be on the south side of the road. Press the button on the electronic gate and identify yourself.

Money Matters: A week at The Golden Door costs $2,500 per person, including everything except private tennis lessons, haircuts and re-styling, and state room tax. The Golden Door accepts MasterCard and Visa.

Observations: This is a spa that means busi-ness. Don't come here if you want pampering and nothing else. Also, keep in mind that once you arrive, you remain within The Golden Door confines for a week. No one chains you in, but slipping out for a movie or shopping expedition in nearby San Diego is not encouraged. Nor is escaping for a pizza. Don't do as some have and bring candy. Do come with bathing suits, tights and leotards, and a few casual dresses or slacks outfits if you feel you will tire of The Golden Door wardrobe. On the last night, everyone gener-ally puts on makeup and a pretty dress for the final supper.

140

The Golden Door

19 *Ingleside Inn*

Palm Springs, California

T o the early Indians and Mexicans, the patch of palm-covered desert at the edge of the San Jacinto Mountains was known as *La Palma de la Mano de Dios*, "the hollow of God's hand." Over the years, God's hand developed a Midas touch in these parts. The area that eventually came to be called Palm Springs is one of those worldly watering spots where the statistics sound fanciful, even absurd, yet are true. Palm Springs is a community of 32,000 residents and 3,000 millionaires whose combined income is said to be $60 billion. (Unlike Palm Beach, it doesn't much matter in Palm Springs how or when one got his money.) Palm Springs boasts more television sets and telephones than people, and if everyone in town jumped into a pool at the same time, there would be only four swimmers in each. There are 54 golf courses in the area, 36 country clubs, 27 public tennis courts and approximately 300 private ones. The average temperature in February is 72 degrees and the average age is about 42. The smells are of oleander and jasmine, the sounds are the whack of golf balls and the clink of ice, which explains the local saying that the air in Palm Springs is 99 percent (smogless) oxygen and 1 percent martini.

Palm Springs, of course, is not everyone's taste. It is rather like liver and onions, or New Wave rock: people love it or hate it. The jagged, barren mountains can look about as romantic as strip-mined Appalachian peaks in the harsh light of the midday sun. The endless vistas of sand meeting cloudless sky make some visitors nervous, as if they were confronting eternity head on. These are the people who escape to lusher terrain like Palm Beach or Maui, leaving Palm Springs to devotees of the desert. "There is a tranquility here," says a transplanted San Franciscan who has bid a blissful farewell to fog, smog, and rain. "There is peace of mind."

This intangible peace has also lured a celebrity contingent. Over the years, Palm Springs has become Hollywood's sandy backyard. The *H* made out of blue tile still stands on the gate of the house Barbara Hutton bought for Cary Grant; the bars still remain on the windows of Elvis Presley's estate. Bob Hope's hillside mansion is a landmark, as is Liberace's place, with the candlelabra held up by a cherub out front. Frank Sinatra, Suzanne Sommers, Kirk Douglas, and Mary Martin own property in the community. The Palm Springs area is also, of course, an adopted hometown for Walter Annenberg and Gerald Ford. And Dwight Eisenhower once made the 11th fairway at El Dorado Country Club his winter home.

In this playground for millionaires, movie stars, and statesmen, hotel and re-

142

Ingleside Inn

sort complexes are, naturally, abundant. Many offer luxury, but not the cachet the discerning Palm Springs visitor seeks, even demands. One that does is Ingleside Inn, a small, historic estate that operates more like a manor house than a resort.

Ingleside is the kind of place a British governor might have inhabited in North Africa or Ceylon. Behind its scrolled wrought-iron gates and white stucco walls there is a sultriness. It's not so much the perfume of the flowers climbing over the wooden trellis on the front porch. Nor is it, specifically, the sleepy central courtyard where a sparrow drinks from the lily pond and a cypress shades the lovers on a stone bench. Romance, intangible but pervasive, is in the air. If Ingleside weren't a hotel, it would have served well as a movie set. One can almost imagine Humphrey Bogart and Lauren Bacall wandering past the heavy wood doors, shuttered windows, and Edwardian portraits in dark oak frames that line the walls along the perimeter of the courtyard.

The real-life habitués, mostly southern California lawyers, doctors, and businessmen, think of Ingleside the way the English do of La Mamounia Hotel in Marrakesh. Like Winston Churchill's beloved La Mamounia, it is an oasis in the desert, a haven where propriety is as important as comfort. Noisy children and radios are banned from Ingleside's swimming pools. (Families with kids stay at a nearby apartment-hotel complex under the same management.) Watercress and mustard sandwiches are served at dart matches on the lawn near the gazebo. A slim volume of short stories by O. Henry rests by one's bedside. In the small lobby, more like a church vestry with its altar lamps, Flemish tapestry, and refectory table, no one speaks loudly.

Ingleside guests tend to lie lifeless by the pool like lazy desert tortoises. They sit in the adjacent hot tub and watch the San Jacinto Mountains turn purple in the fading afternoon light. They play backgammon on the veranda or shuffleboard under the acacia tree. The Hollywood screenwriters who drift in and out of Ingleside hole up at a desk in one of the stucco cottages or bungalows spread out around the property. Movie stars pluck oranges from their patio and sip champagne in air-conditioned privacy. A sheik who arrived with an entourage of bodyguards, servants, and children (an exeption to the "no kids" rule was made) enjoyed a candlelit, Middle Eastern dinner in his quarters.

In its earlier years, Ingleside attracted a far stuffier bunch. The inn dates back to 1925, when it was built as a mansion for Humphrey Birge, an heir to the Pierce Arrow fortune. Worldly types, the Birges entertained lavishly and filled their home with an unusual collection of antiques. The sienna bust of Petrarch's Laura bought by the Birges still stands in the lobby. Their carved wooden storage chest, said to have belonged to Mary, Queen of Scots, is out on the porch. The real character of Ingleside, however, was established by a

Ingleside Inn

widowed Indiana Hoosier. Ruth Hardy arrived in Palm Springs one day and immediately made her presence known. It was Hardy who, as Palm Springs's first councilwoman, came up with the idea of putting lighted palms along Palm Canyon Drive, the main street. Determined to be an innkeeper, too, she bought Ingleside in 1935 and set about turning it into a private club for the right paying guests. Lily Pons came so many times that special quarters were set aside for her and furnished in her favorite peach velvets and tufted satins. Andre Kostelanetz, Greta Garbo, and Salvador Dali also frequented Ingleside. The reclusive Howard Hughes courted Ava Gardner at the inn, and Carole Lombard and Clark Gable honeymooned there.

The proper proprietress loved all the glitter, but frowned on certain guests. In fact, years after her death in 1965, a card-index file was found that amounted to a secret dossier on Ingleside's clientele. Hardy made careful notations about the physical appearances and occupations of those who registered at her inn. She disliked guests who were loud, pushy, foreign (with the exception of the English and Northern Europeans), shacking up, or of the wrong ethnic backgrounds. Hence, producer Sam Goldwyn's card read "N.G." (for No Good) and "J" (for Jewish), as did Mervyn LeRoy's. Howard Hughes, who checked in as "Earl Martyn" when he arrived with Ava Gardner ("Mrs. Clark") was defi-

nitely an N.G. Of course, Hardy did approve of *some* guests. Elizabeth Taylor was "a lovely young girl." Greer Garson was "O.K. — lovely actress," as was Pola Negri. Also on Hardy's O.K. list: Bette Davis, Katharine Hepburn, Rita Hayworth, and Cyd Charisse.

When the Hardy era ended, Ingleside grew ramshackle. The celebrities found tonier hangouts. Then, one day in 1975, a Brooklyn-born businessman in his late thirties arrived in town. Mel Haber had traded a successful career as a manufacturer of angora dice, hula dolls, religious statues, and other automotive novelties for the life of a California drifter. One day a friend dropped by Haber's Palm Springs condominium and suggested that Mel come along while he looked at a possible land investment. The property was Ingleside Inn, run-down but functioning. "I walked in wearing my cutoffs and saw twenty or twenty-five couples, average age sixty-five, sitting there having tea," Haber recalls. "There was no air conditioning and they were all sitting around in suits and ties and dressy clothes. I thought to myself: 'This must be a movie set.'"

Whatever it was, it triggered something in Haber. Within 30 minutes he had bought the place and made plans to turn it into a private playground for himself and his friends and associates. "It would be a place where they could invite their girlfriends or Aunt Tillys," he says. "I had no notion at first of turning Ingleside into a hotel or a restaurant."

Gradually, however, Haber began thinking that he could make Ingleside a superb little hotel, and reclaim some of its former glory in the process. He spent months, and a small fortune, renovating, landscaping, and air-conditioning the inn. He dug through its attics and basements to find the antiques and oil paintings collected in the Birge era. He hired decorators to purchase yet more pieces and incorporate everything into an environment of highly styled traditionalism. The old rooms and bungalows were redone in sophisticated chintzes and velvets and accented with sprays of silk flowers. When it came time to refurbish the restaurant, Haber was concerned that it have an identity. Decorating it in chocolate tones (later changed to striking navy floral prints) was easy. Finding a name wasn't. Calling it "Mel's" was out. "Melvyn's" sounded good, but Haber felt he needed a Melvyn at the door. "*I* wasn't Melvyn," he says. "I've never been called Melvyn. I'm Mel." He looked around unsuccessfully for an employee to fill the bill, and ended up doing it himself.

For his opening night, Haber selected a September evening, not knowing that September was considered a dead month in Palm Springs. Still, the curious locals came in black tie and evening dresses, eager to see what this crazy New Yorker had wrought. Among the first guests to appear was a scruffy fellow on a motorcycle and his pretty companion. Haber took one look and pleaded: "Please. Some other time, pal. This is a special night." The pair obliged. Later, Haber learned that he had turned away Steve McQueen and Ali McGraw.

Within weeks the celebrities were pulling up in their limos. Frank Sinatra and Barbara Marx selected Melvyn's for their pre-wedding dinner in 1976. June Allyson married Dr. David Ashrow in the garden. Marlon Brando drove up in a four-wheel jeep wearing jeans, boots, a cowboy hat, and a sweatband, and was almost refused a room. A desk clerk, fortunately, recognized the voice. (Brando reportedly spent much of his time at Ingleside sitting in his jeep talking on his CB radio.) Not long after Debbie Reynolds called Haber to arrange a 50th birthday party for herself at Ingleside, ex-spouse Eddie Fisher rang up for a room at the same time. Haber deftly persuaded him to come a week earlier. Mary Martin dropped in with friends to sing around the piano in Melvyn's. "It's a wonderful place, she says. "It's kind of like years ago when people liked to sing *songs*."

Ingleside's staff, two per every guest, is obligingly fun-loving. On Bastille Day they prepare a French feast on the lawn. On St. Patrick's Day they drag in a boulder from the desert so that anyone Irish can kiss Palm Springs's version of the Blarney Stone. And any time of the year, they try to pamper their clientele. If a guest ordered a pitcher of bullshots on his last visit, he will likely find one waiting in the room. The refrigerator in every accommodation is stocked (gratis) with juices, sodas, cookies, and cheese. Matches with a guest's name embossed in gold are neatly laid out on a table. The grandmotherly general manager, Babs (Grannie) Rosen, will pack a picnic basket filled with Cornish pasties for those going horseback riding. Should a shopping trip to downtown Palm Springs be in order, a vintage 1956 Rolls-Royce that once belonged to an English lord is waiting with a driver. As one sinks into the leather seats and glides beneath Ruth Hardy's palms, it is easy to understand a comment made by Bob Hope. "Nobody dies in Palm Springs," the comedian once said. "If it looks like they're going to, they do the decent thing and go to San Bernardino."

200 West Ramon
Palm Springs, California 92262

Telephone
714-325-0046

On the Premises: Located only a few blocks from downtown Palm Springs, Ingleside maintains an aura of seclusion. Although it is hardly a typical resort in that it has no golf, tennis, or horseback riding on the property, it does offer ready access to the majority of the 54 golf courses and 36 country clubs in the Palm Springs area. Guests are ferried to their favorite clay or hard-surface tennis courts and to the golf course of their choice. Riding is available at nearby Smoketree Stables. At Ingleside itself, there is a swimming pool with adjacent whirlpool bath, shuffleboard, croquet, and various game facilities.

Rooms: Virtually every one of the 28 guests rooms and suites has its own special charms. Brass beds, Jacobean dark wood mirrors, burnished armoires, and antique marble-topped tables are spread here and there. Manager Babs Rosen hunts for prints from *Godey's Lady's Book* to put on the walls, and crochets scarves for the dressers. She also has an affection for lace curtains and floral chintzes. In every bath there is a whirlpool and steambath. Of all the accommodations at Ingleside, perhaps the most romantic is the Lily Pons Room, where the diva slept. Honeymooners are often ensconced here amidst the Louis Quinze furniture, the velvets, and laces. The most lavish suite at Ingleside is the Royal Suite (a favorite with John Travolta, Cindy Williams, and Barry Goldwater, Jr.). The vaulted living room is furnished with gray velvet Queen Anne chairs and Oriental rugs. One of the two baths has a sunken marble tub, a bidet, and a vanity that stretches wall to wall.

147

Meals: Before going to bed, fill out the breakfast form and hang it on your door. The next morning at the requested time, the waiter will arrive with a complimentary breakfast of freshly squeezed orange juice, croissants, and Danish. (A full breakfast is also available for an additional charge.) At lunchtime, Melvyn's offers continental entrees such as steaks, crepes, and veal scallopini, as well as salad platters, sandwiches, and burgers. In the evening, waiters in ruffled shirts and dinner jackets preside over the candlelit dining room. The appetizer selection includes fettucine tetrazzini (noodles tossed with cream, cheeses, chicken, ham and sherried mushrooms), beluga caviar, pâté with truffles, and escargots. Among the entrees are Spanish prawns, lobster thermidor, tournedos Melvyn, and steak Diane. The cinnamon apple or chocolate chip cheesecake are standouts at dessert, but nothing tops the chocolate mousse pie imported from La Mousse Factory in Los Angeles.

Getting There: The Palm Springs Municipal Airport is a 10-minute drive from the inn, and pickup service (sometimes in the hotel's Rolls) is available. If driving from Los Angeles, take Interstate 10 to the Palm Springs exit, which turns into Palm Canyon Drive; stay on Palm Canyon until Ramon; turn right on Ramon and go one block to the inn.

Money Matters: Ingleside operates on the European plan and includes a Continental breakfast and stocked refrigerator in the price of the room. In the high season (October 1 to June 1) a double room begins at $85; suites range from $135 to $500. Summer rates range from $45 for a double to $95 to $300 for a suite. The inn accepts MasterCard, Visa, and American Express.

Side Trips: Sun and sports are most sought after here, but sightseeing is available if you want it. The Desert Museum and Moorten's Botanical Gardens give a good introduction to desert flora and fauna. The Palm Springs Aerial Tramway, which carries 80 people from the desert to an 8,516 elevation on Mount San Jacinto in 14 minutes, is perhaps the most visited attraction.

Observations: Ingleside is a small gem in a glitzy setting. Owner Haber wants couples, not families, at the inn in the belief that Ingleside is a romantic spot for escaping and trysting. Families with children are referred to the Royal Aire, a separate complex of eight two-bedroom suites and one villa under the same ownership. (Guests at the Royal Aire have full use of all Ingleside facilities.)

148

Ingleside Inn

Melvyn's restaurant.

20 *San Ysidro Ranch*

Montecito, California

One cloudless August evening in 1940, a famous English actor and a dark-haired English actress fresh from her American triumph in *Gone With the Wind* stood on a rose-covered terrace overlooking the Pacific. "I do," murmured Laurence Olivier. "I do," said Vivien Leigh. As Katharine Hepburn and Garson Kanin looked on as witnesses, the pair were proclaimed man and wife. "Is that all?" wondered the bride, surprised at the brevity of the simple service in the hills of Montecito. Soon, she and her new husband motored off toward Santa Monica and a honeymoon on actor Ronald Colman's schooner, *Dragoon*.

Thirteen years later, another handsome couple strolled hand in hand through the tangled gardens and orange groves of San Ysidro Ranch. John and Jacqueline Kennedy selected this rustic retreat for a portion of their honeymoon. The young senator and his bride hid from the world in a stone cottage furnished with English chintzes and overgrown with grapevines.

Over the decades, the rough-cut charms of San Ysidro have lured a band of polished and high-gloss visitors. To the Hollywood crowd, part of the appeal in the early years was the owner, Ronald Colman. The actor often summoned pals like Groucho Marx, Bing Crosby, and Jack Benny to drive up from Los Angeles, sip Scotch, and enjoy San Ysidro's jasmine-scented air. Writers, too, found the ranch's crumbling walls an inspiration. Somerset Maugham penned several short stories at San Ysidro. Sinclair Lewis pounded on his typewriter in a dressing-room closet. "I can't write looking out at that beautiful ocean," he once said. "It would be too distracting. I would lose my characters." John Galsworthy, who revised *The Forsyte Saga* at the ranch, was so moved by its peacefulness that in 1921 he wrote an "Ode to San Ysidro": "How beautiful! When the woodsmoke goes up straight, and the pepper trees stand unswerving, and behind the screen of the tall Eucalyptus trees, the fallen sun glows, a lone slow fire over the sea, and the lavender-colored mist rises between . . . well may it be sainted, San Ysidro."

The ranch that stirred such passion in the heart of an Englishman still beckons sensitive souls: writers (mostly screenwriters nowadays), actors, and lovers, who can be seen clutching hands by the rosebushes. Ronald Colman, who died in 1958, would be pleased to find that the new owners, Jim Lavenson, a former president of Manhattan's Plaza Hotel, and his wife, Susie, have not changed the character of San Ysidro. They have managed to redecorate, refurbish, and replumb the old hotel without destroying its innate ragtag charm. Hollywood types seem to appreciate coming here as a respite from the world of glitter. Without a second's thought, they drive the 100 miles for Sunday brunch, or a candlelight dinner. One night in the restaurant, Mike Douglas, John Travolta, and Steve Martin were all enjoying their dinner at separate tables. "Everybody else stopped eating," recalls Robert Lopez, San Ysidro's maître d'. Other famous personalities bunk down at the ranch for a few days, or even a few weeks. Barbra Streisand, who came for about a week, jogged around the grounds each morning in shorts and an electric-blue jacket. Gore Vidal, Richard Widmark, Burt Reynolds and Sally Fields, John Ritter, and Joanne Woodward and Paul Newman have all savored this scruffy hideaway.

Each guest, famous or not, is welcomed by the sight of his last name spelled out in wooden letters on a sign outside his door. Naturally, given the clientele, the management will gladly substitute an "anonymous" sign upon request. Curiously enough for a resort touted by *Los Angeles* magazine in an article entitled: "Where and When to Have That Affair," ("nearly bustproof" was the verdict), few request anonymity. Hence, the "Williams" would likely be Paul and the "Child" Julia and her husband, Paul. "It's a beautiful place on the breast of the mountains," says Mrs. Child. "It's one of the nicest places we've been . . . very informal and outdoorsy. In fact, we have bought a small apartment nearby. We've grown to love the area mainly thanks to our stays at San Ysidro."

To the uninitiated, a first glimpse of the ranch can be disconcerting. The curving country road leading to San Ysidro dead-ends at an unimposing white clapboard main building (called the hacienda). Folksy yellow-and-white-striped awnings flutter when the wind picks up. On the porch, for no apparent reason, stands a whimsical wooden hobby horse. The straw door mat reads: "Meanwhile. . . ."

151

The main building, or "hacienda."

San Ysidro Ranch

The ranch's 19, one- and two-bedroom cottages reflect this same down-home touch. "People come here for rustic elegance, not for marble baths and tubs shaped like a leaf," says Susie Lavenson, who does the decorating. She unabashedly admits that she frequents such establishments as the Salvation Army and J.C. Penney for furniture and fabrics. Invariably, she returns to the ranch with a charming Victorian settee, a brass fireplace fender, or a pretty chintz bedspread. Of all Susie's touches, she is proudest, perhaps, of the baths, each of which has an old wooden bureau plumbed as a sink. The tubs, however, are all brand new and equipped with hydromassage shower heads.

For those who require more than charm and fancy shower heads, there are the vistas. Each cottage faces either the Santa Ynez Mountains or the distant Pacific. In six of the cottages, guests can stare at the scenery from the privacy of their own hot tub enclosed on a redwood deck. Terry robes are gladly supplied, but not, to one guest's chagrin, gardenias for floating in the bubbles.

Given the virtues of these cottages, some guests rarely emerge. (The management jokes that it force-feeds anyone who doesn't come out for 24 hours.) In fact, the demands for privacy are so great that the Lavensons discontinued a nightly bed turndown because a number of guests said they didn't want to be disturbed.

Room service, naturally, is highly popular at the ranch. But the restaurant, too, does a brisk business. Called the Plow and Angel, it was once an old citrus packinghouse. Inside its white stone walls, a series of dining areas provide secluded corners for trysting. Susie Lavenson's touch is again evident in the Early American cabinet once used for drying bacon, and in the leaded-glass screen purchased at a crafts fair on the beach. On the walls are framed color photographs of the Montecito countryside taken by Paul Child, a talented nature photographer.

Julia Child vouches for the food. "They're trying very hard, and they are succeeding," she says. Mrs. Child was especially impressed to learn that the Lavensons had sent their chef, Wendy Little, to France's famed cooking school, La Varenne. Wendy's dishes, which she describes as "Continental with emphasis on nouvelle cuisine," are always followed by an exotic 30-inch long napoleon (filled with rum and kiwis one day, raspberries and brandy the next). The creator of this and other confections is Wendy's younger sister, Anne, the ranch's pastry chef.

Years ago San Ysidro was a way station for a very different breed of traveler: the Franciscan monks. The Spanish padres had come to California in the late eighteenth century, and they built 21 missions from San Diego to Sonoma. The 10th mission, founded in 1786, was in Santa Barbara, a few miles from Montecito. Among the holdings of the Santa Barbara missionaries was San Ysidro, a working citrus and cattle ranch. Over the years the ranch fell into the hands of private families, who built simple stone-and-wood cottages. By 1883 San Ysidro had become a small guest ranch.

The Colman era began in 1934 and is best remembered by Alvin Weingand, a former California state senator who, for many years, was the actor's friend and business partner. Weingand and Colman first met in 1928 at the Pine Inn in Carmel, California. At the time, Weingand was working as a desk clerk. Colman, a guest at the inn, befriended the young clerk. "Colman loved quiet, nice places, playing tennis, and drinking Scotch," recalls Weingand. "One day, he confided in me that his dream was to have an anchor in this world, a beautiful, remote place. I told him that *my* ambition was to have a little hotel someday." The pair soon decided to find the right spot and open a hotel. After considerable searching and wandering through Europe, they heard that the old San Ysidro Ranch was on the market, and they quickly bought it. "It was always genteely crummy," remembers Weingand. "The vines would grow through holes in the walls, and we started to cut them down. But people who lived in Hollywood mansions begged us not to. They said they *liked* it that way. So we left the vines alone."

During the 28 years of their partnership, Weingand served as the resident manager at San Ysidro while Colman pursued his acting career. Ronald and his wife, Benita, maintained a house on the property and visited whenever possible. Under the Colman-Weingand management, the atmosphere was one of unpretentious conviviality. And the price was right. In 1935 two people could stay in a private cottage with full bath and living room, and eat three meals a day, for $14. "Drinks were always on the house," says Weingand. "We didn't open a bar until 1955. Nobody *wanted* one."

With its free booze and quiet charm, San Ysidro became a favorite hangout for Hollywood producers and directors who wanted to sneak away for a weekend with their spouse — or favorite starlet. The management never fretted much about technicalities like marriage licenses. "We never let our moral attitude interfere with the *business* aspect of things," recalls Weingand.

154

San Ysidro Ranch

After Colman's death in 1958, San Ysidro slipped into a bleak era of financial woes and disrepair. Enter Jim and Susie Lavenson. Jim is a Philadelphia-born Williams College graduate whose family advertising business, the Lavenson Bureau of Advertising, was hired by Manhattan's Plaza Hotel. Gradually, Lavenson learned more and more about the hotel business through his work at the Plaza. In 1971 he was named president of the Plaza, a position he equates with "being king of England." In 1975 the Plaza was sold to Westin Hotels, and Lavenson decided he wanted to buy his own resort. After his efforts to purchase the Santa Barbara Biltmore did not succeed, he was told about San Ysidro. "I had never seen anything so contaminated. I was afraid to get out of the car," he recalls of his first glimpse of the ranch. But Lavenson and his wife figured they could beautify San Ysidro. In 1976 they purchased the ranch and started a long-range modernization. "Those first few months we were open, it looked so bad I wanted to wear a catcher's mask at the front desk," remembers Jim.

Today, Lavenson stands tall in Western shirt and dusty boots. Yet the dude from the East hasn't totally abandoned his city-slicker past. All over San Ysidro are reminders that a former adman runs the show. "Gentlemen must wear jackets, and please remove your spurs before going to bed," reads the sign outside the dining-room door. On the bedside telephone in the cottages is a little sticker saying: "Dial 210 (and talk to a horse). Help, and lesser problems, dial 0." The restaurant wine list urges patrons to "save water . . . drink expensive old wines." Those sober enough to stroll the grounds after dinner stumble upon yet another of Lavenson's touches. A discreet sign on San Ysidro's greenhouse admonishes visitors: "Quiet, please. Flowers mating."

900 San Ysidro Lane
Montecito, California　93108

Telephone
805-969-5046

On the Premises: This unpretentious resort tucked away in the foothills of the Santa Ynez Mountains offers 38 accommodations, many in secluded cottages. Although the average guest comes simply to get away in a highly romantic setting, a few do want sporting facilities. The ranch has three tennis courts on a terraced hillside, a large heated pool, a stable stocked with approximately nine horses (lessons and daily trail rides into the mountains are available), as well as croquet, Ping-Pong, and badminton. Golf can be arranged at a nearby club.

Rooms: Each one has its own distinct touches and name. In Acacia there is hand-screened stencil-print wallpaper, a Franklin stove, and an antique breakfront. Forest, an old stableman's shack, is now a one-bedroom suite with a kitchen and private hot tub. In Willow III, an enormous, one-bedroom suite, the living room is furnished with ladder-back chairs, Japanese woodcuts, and a brocade settee.

Meals: Start the day with freshly squeezed orange juice (it comes regular or "glutton size"), brandied French toast, or perhaps cheese blintzes. Lunches at the ranch include salads, quiches, sandwiches, and light entrees. Dinner is the highlight. Chef Wendy Little prepares such imaginative dishes as local prawns with mangoes and green peppercorns, veal chops stuffed with apples, pecans, and

155

sage, and steamed salmon with a basil and saffron beurre blanc. Pastry Chef Anne Little specializes in papaya tortes, chocolate cream banana cake, and her nightly napoleon.

Getting There: The nearest airport is in Santa Barbara, about 20 minutes from the hotel. Driving, San Ysidro is less than two hours north of Los Angeles on Route 101. Take the San Ysidro Road exit just south of Santa Barbara; go right and follow the signs. (The ranch is approximately 2 miles from the freeway exit.)

Money Matters: Say Ysidro is strictly on the European plan. The simplest double goes for about $98. Suites begin at $149, and individual cottages start at $189. A cottage with private hot tub ranges from $239 to $345. The ranch accepts MasterCard, Visa, and American Express.

San Ysidro Ranch

Side Trips: Montecito, an affluent community where movie stars live behind stone fences, is a lovely place for a drive. So is nearby Santa Barbara, a picturesque seaside town with red tiled roofs and terrazzo walls. Visitors might also want to tour the Santa Barbara Mission. A one-hour drive over the Santa Ynez Mountains takes you to Solvang, a small Danish-American village with windmills, gas streetlights from Copenhagen, and a Lutheran church.

Observations: "No one should come to San Ysidro for the first time," jokes co-owner Susie Lavenson. "They don't know what to expect." Indeed, San Ysidro is unprepossessing at first glance: a down-home, friendly place where the worldly are encouraged to kick off fancy clothes and simply relax. Although the ranch offers sufficient sports facilities, it is more of a retreat than a grand-scale resort. The rooms are whimsical and folksy, not slick.

21 *Sonoma Mission Inn*

Boyes Hot Springs, California

On a hot, sleepy Friday the 13th in June 1980, a businessman in his early forties hovered nervously in the lobby of his new hotel. The $8 million renovations were completed, the staff was at hand, and the shell pink flag was fluttering nicely above the freshly painted shell pink exterior. "All we needed was our first guest," Edward J. Safdie recalls of his Sonoma Mission Inn's opening day. Finally, a Rolls-Royce pulled up and a driver in full livery jumped out to open the door. "The passenger was in his fifties with a full head of gray hair and a Palm Beach tan. He walked to the reception desk and checked in. If we could have picked the perfect guest from Central Casting, we would have picked *him*," says Safdie.

Before long, the Rollses, Jaguars, and Porsches were parked fender to fender along the circular driveway. At first, the crowd, mostly from San Francisco, came out of curiosity, hearing that some brash developer had turned the historic but run-down old inn into a glitzy resort. Gradually, they began returning and passing the word to friends in Los Angeles, New York, even Europe. Only an hour from San Francisco in the middle of the wine country, they reported, is a resort with good tennis, an Olympic-size pool surrounded by cabanas, a space-age health spa, and innovative nouvelle cuisine. Best of all, noted some, the Sonoma Mission Inn had managed to avoid the cutesy Victorian decor popular with the little inns and bed-and-breakfast places in the area. No flocked wallpaper, flowered chintzes, or brass beds were to be seen. Instead, the late San Francisco designer John Dickinson had decorated the inn in a haut deco style reminiscent of nothing else.

"We knew they would either love it or hate it, but at least they'd talk about it," says Safdie. Early on he made the decision to paint the inn's dirty, tannish facade a blushing pink. "It's a mellow, soft, nonoffensive color," he explains. "It's hard to be nasty to someone in a pink shirt. Besides, it's a *resort* color." And, no, he insists, he was not trying to imitate the rosy Beverly Hills Hotel.

For the interior of the two-story hotel, built in 1927 in the mission revival style, Dickinson worked in cool earth tones. In the lobby, a baronial 40 × 80-foot room scaled for a castle, he emphasized the size of the hall with sparse furnishings. A few overstuffed roll-arm chairs, a sofa, and puffed divans-in-the-round are fringed and upholstered in dove gray velours. Wrought-iron floor lamps and a reindeer statue add to the panache of what Dickinson called "country chic." In the two wings of the hotel, he renovated and replumbed the 97 rooms and 5 suites. Using three basic color schemes, camel, taupe, and terra-cotta, he managed to integrate flair (plantation shutters on the windows

158

Sonoma Mission Inn

and soaring half-canopies over the beds) and function (adjustable reading lights above the pillows and swiveling pine tables that conceal clock radio, telephone, and television). "Essentially," says Safdie, "they're rooms for the practical-minded aesthete."

The aesthetes are of two breeds, the tourists and the guests who are participating in one of the programs offered by the spa at the Sonoma Mission Inn. You can tell the former by their vacation tans, their well-pressed slacks, the Ralph Lauren sweaters tossed over their shoulders, and their willingness to gorge themselves in the restaurant. You will immediately notice their "let's-not-miss-a-thing" attitude. This is well-evidenced at the concierge's desk, where they cluster around seeking advice on how to get into invitation-only vineyards (usually a telephone call will do the job), or whether to try one of the reputedly therapeutic mud baths in the Napa town of Calistoga (yes, if you like sitting in a tub of mud prepared from the black volcanic ash in the soil).

As for the spa guests, you won't see much of them. They spend most of their time behind locked gates in a separate building a few steps from the hotel. (In the old days, the spa was the site of a Quonset hut that housed the Boyes Hot Springs porno parlor.) When you see a spa guest in the lobby, you will immediately recognize the gray warm-up suits with pink stripes on the arms and the lean hungry look. Should you overhear a conversation, it will likely be about

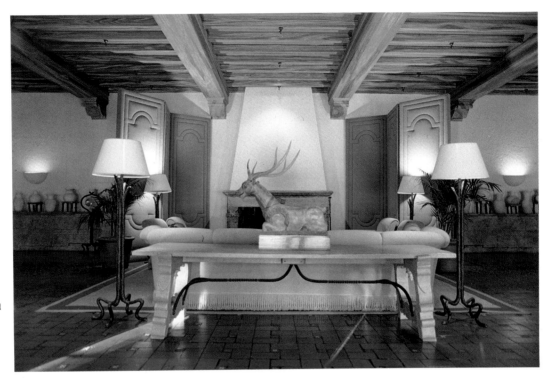

The entrance to the spa framed by sprayed manzanita branches (*left*) and a view of the lobby (*right*).

161

food: what they're having for supper, what the *wish* they were having for supper, and whether or not they should slip over to the soda fountain across the street for a sundae. Almost no one does. As one guest puts it: "Why spend all that money, then blow it?"

The program that inspires such restraint lasts three to five days (special weekend arrangements are also possible). Generally, the spa is for women only, but the opposite sex invades on certain men's weeks. A typical day at the spa begins with a 5:45 wake-up call in one's room at the inn. Then comes a 2- to 4-mile walk through nearby Jack London State Forest. Later, while the regular hotel guests are breakfasting leisurely on coffee and croissants (rumored to be about 500 calories each), the spa clientele are hard at work in calisthenics or aerobics classes.

The staff, headed by Eva Jensch, takes special pride in the hydrotherapy program. Guests climb into custom-made turquoise-and-white tubs filled with warm mineral water. A trained therapist then massages nearly every part of the body with water jets and a pressurized hose. The aim, explains Jensch, is to stimulate circulation, break down cellulite, even improve kidney and liver function. Another specialty is the cleansing herbal wrap in which one is swathed in linen sheets soaked in odd combinations of lavender, peppermint, sassafras, chamomile, mugwort, and other plants. To avoid boredom during the wrap, the staff offers taped nature sounds or disco music.

Later, the guest sheds the sheets and sweat suits and puts on civilian clothes (slacks or a casual skirt) for dinner. The setting is a private, candlelit salon painted the pink of (forbidden) peppermint-stick ice cream. The china is an elegant flowered pattern from Villeroy & Boch. Wielding gold-plated forks and knives, the diners dig into beautifully garnished entrees such as curried chicken en brochette (200 calories) or seafood quenelle (170 calories). For dessert there is an airy mousse or perhaps lo-cal cheesecake. The daily calorie total, including three meals and juice breaks, is about 800. Because this, after all, is grape country, the women are even invited to a predinner wine tasting one night during their stay and allowed to consume a few precious ounces.

In the inn's regular dining room, called Provençal, both food and wine are consumed with bacchanalian abandon. Provençal is the pride of the hotel, a pink hideaway where one can live *la vie culinaire en rose*. The same chef who meticulously weighs and measures the ingredients of the spa cuisine (under the guidance of a resident nutritionist) abandons all restraints when it comes to the restaurant. Lawrence Elbert, who has cooked at London's Connaught Hotel, the Hotel D'Angleterre in Copenhagen, and Manhattan's River Café, prides himself on being different. If baked Brie, stuffed snow peas, or kiwi tarts are the culinary rage of the moment, Elbert will avoid them. Instead, he serves French provincial and a few Italian dishes that owe as much to northern California as they do to Europe. Oysters from Bodega Bay, Sacramento delta crayfish, Petaluma-raised poultry and game, and mushrooms from the local woods are used liberally. To accompany Elbert's cuisine, the management has prepared a list of wines grown only in Sonoma County. (Imported champagnes are allowed.)

This reflects the inn's chauvinism about the Sonoma Valley. A growing rivalry exists between Napa, the traditional haunt of wine-tasting tourists, and Sonoma, which has more recently come into its own. "Napa is becoming the Disneyland of the wine country," says Safdie. "It has McDonald's and Kentucky Fried Chicken. Sonoma is reverse chic. It is still a rural place."

Viticulture in the Sonoma valley dates back to the early 1800s, when Spanish friars planted grapes for sacramental wine near their Mission San Francisco Solano. Later, the hot, dry days and cool nights attracted other Europeans eager to establish vineyards in the fertile volcanic soil. As more and more vintners settled in the tiny valley, the town of Sonoma developed into a thriving business center. It was in historic Sonoma that the short-lived California Republic was born with the raising of the Bear Flag in 1846.

162

**Sonoma
Mission Inn**

In a hamlet 2 miles to the north, the soil yielded other riches. Bubbling hot springs in the area had been discovered centuries earlier by the northern California Indian tribes. In the late nineteenth-century, Captain Henry Ernest Boyes, an Englishman who had purchased a 75-acre site in this countryside, was poking around on his land. He eventually struck a well of hot water. A resourceful sort, he quickly constructed a bathhouse on the site, then a hotel. The local citizenry named the town Boyes Hot Springs after this ambitious newcomer. Soon, Boyes Hot Springs was a fashionable spa for visiting San Franciscans. Then, in 1923, a fire destroyed much of the community, including Captain Boyes's hotel. A new establishment was soon built. Capitalizing on the tourist interest in the nearby California missions, it was named the Sonoma Mission Inn.

The genteel resort town was to disintegrate during the era of Prohibition. Slot machines, speakeasies, and emporiums run by Spanish Kitty and her ilk abounded. After repeal, however, the town regained some of its respectability. The Sonoma Mission Inn once again prospered. Ironically, a young boy named Edward Safdie, son of a San Francisco importer, vacationed in the area with his family in the 50s, but stayed at a less-expensive motel. "My father was prudent," he says.

In 1979, when Safdie heard that the old inn was on the market, he moved quickly. By then he had become a well-established developer of real estate in New York and San Francisco, and felt he knew a good investment when he saw it. The run-down old inn, Safdie was sure, could be turned into a California classic. Moreover, he says, "I felt instinctively that the wine country would be 'it' for the next decade."

So far, Safdie's intuition is proving correct. The roads of Sonoma and Napa are bumper to bumper on weekends (try to go on weekdays if you can and visit the wineries in the morning). Moreover, the area is attracting its share of resident celebrities like Robin Williams, Pat Paulsen, and the Smothers Brothers, some of whom are even in the wine business. Other show-business personalities fly up from Hollywood to tour the wineries. The local grocery in the little town of Oakville, where many stop for picnic lunches, has become a popular celebrity-watching spot.

Many of the visiting stars register at the Sonoma Mission Inn. Margaux Hemingway, Valerie Perrine, and Olivia de Havilland have all sweated through the spa (de Havilland booked for one week and stayed for three). For owner Ed Safdie, the most exciting visitor was probably the comptroller who strode into his office one day and announced that the inn was in the black—a mere 18 months after opening.

18141 Sonoma Highway
Boyes Hot Springs, California   95416

Telephone
707-996-1041

On the Premises: Located in a region of bed-and-breakfast places and quaint country inns, Sonoma Mission Inn is a sophisticated, full-service resort that serves as a good base for exploring the wine country. The inn has a pool with five cabanas, three tennis courts (two are lighted for night play) and golf privileges at a nearby country club; hot-air ballooning, a popular sport in the area, can be arranged by the concierge. The spa at Sonoma Mission Inn caters to 15 to 30 women (and offers occasional men's weeks). Considered one of the most advanced spas in the nation, it has a gym equipped with pneumatic resistance machines (similar to Nautilus equipment, except that they use compressed air rather than weights and pulleys to create the resistance factor). Other services at the spa include beauty programs, hydrotherapy, and lectures on self-defense and stress management.

164

Sonoma
Mission Inn

Rooms: All the accommodations are decorated with the same half-canopy beds, modern cubes and chairs, and monochrome colors. A few, however, have unique features. Room 232, located in a tower, is perfectly round and rather charming. The four suites have separate sitting areas; the so-called master suite has a dining room and kitchen as well; five of the rooms open onto terraces. In all accommodations the baths are newly renovated and outfitted with spacious makeup areas and hydromassage shower heads. A separate dressing area with bureau and large closet is located in an alcove off each bedroom.

Meals: A complimentary Continental breakfast is served each morning in the bar. Those who want a full breakfast can cross the street to the Big 3 Fountain, also owned by the inn. Lunch, a fairly casual meal, consists of salads, sandwiches, cold barbecued chicken, and the like, served in the bar or at a poolside grill. In Provençal, the inn's restaurant, specialties include Petaluma duckling flavored with ginger and Madeira, saddle of lamb baked in puff pastry, and boneless trout filled with a smoked-salmon mousse and served with lobster sauce. For dessert, ask for the crème Provençal, a bavaroise flambéed with liqueur and topped with berries, or one of the exotic homemade ice creams (Black Forest or ginger rum) and sorbets (Amaretto peach and blueberry champagne are favorites).

Getting There: The inn makes regular pickups at the San Francisco Airport (advanced reservations are needed). For those negotiating their own way, the inn is 40 miles north of San Francisco and is reached by driving

across the Golden Gate Bridge and continuing on Highway 101 North. On Highway 37 make a right turn; take a left at Highway 121 and go straight until you reach the town of Sonoma. At the town plaza turn left on Highway 12 and continue for about 2 miles.

Money Matters: The inn operates on the European plan, with double rooms ranging from $105 to $175 per night. A five-day spa program (Sunday through Friday) costs $1,800 per person; the three-day program (Sunday through Wednesday) costs $1,100; the weekender (Friday and Saturday nights) is priced at $275 per person. The inn accepts Visa, American Express, and Diners Club.

Side Trips: Days can be spent exploring the winding country roads and touring the wineries. In recent years, countless restaurants have sprung up specializing in dishes sautéed and flambéed in the local wines and spirits. A few are booked weeks, even months, in advance, notably the superb restaurant at Domaine Chandon, the sparkling-wine company. For those enophiles who enjoy history, the Sonoma area is doubly ripe. It was in Sonoma that the Mexican overlord, General Mariano Guadalupe Vallejo, settled with his troops in 1834; the restored barracks as well as the general's home are open to the public. About 10 miles from Sonoma, visitors can tour the remains of another famous residence, Wolf House, novelist Jack London's stone mansion, which burned down before he could move in. The author's ashes are buried beneath a red lava knoll near the ruins.

Observations: With its dramatic facade and groves of sycamore and oak, the inn is a gracious enclave in a town that has seen better days. Keep in mind that the rooms at the inn, though comfortable, are not particularly large. Also the hotel has no air conditioning, only ceiling fans, which do the job nicely on all but the worst summer days. If visiting during a hot spell in July or August, a room on the cooler front side is the best choice. Anytime, come expecting to dress smartly (especially at dinner, where silk slacks and dresses and suits and sports jackets are the norm) and to people-watch by the pool.

165

22 *Salishan Lodge*

Gleneden Beach, Oregon

A limousine winds its way past forests of spruce and Douglas fir and up a hillside to an unpretentious, driftwood-colored lodge. The chauffeur opens the door for a middle-aged man dressed in a plaid flannel jacket, corduroy pants, and knee-high hiking boots. He has left his business and his pin-striped suits behind, and looks forward to a vacation hiking through the woods. Inside the lodge, in the second-floor art gallery, a couple in golf clothes debate whether they should pick up a few abstracts for their collection. Over in the Gourmet Dining Room, as it is called, another couple sips 1961 Château Lafite, one of the 35,000 bottles in the underground wine cellar. They discuss, over chateaubriand, their plans to go fishing the next day for Chinook salmon. Should they catch one, the management will gladly tag and freeze it. "God help us," says Russ Cleveland, the general manager of Salishan Lodge, "if we get it wrong."

On virtually every front, the management of Salishan has a delicate task. It must cater to the needs and whims of its sports-minded guests (Want a guide for duck hunting or crab fishing? Just ask at the front desk) and provide a suitably casual backdrop. Yet it must also give affluent outdoors types (or those merely splurging) the sophistication in comforts, cuisine, even artwork, that they desire. To be *too* elegant would be out of place. To be rustic would be like almost every other place on the Oregon coast. At Salishan they strive, effectively, for a balance.

They also aim to be ecological. The owners, John D. Gray, a Portland industrialist, and his wife, Betty, saw how the coastline to the north of Salishan had been despoiled by unsightly motels, beer joints, and fast-food restaurants. In building Salishan, they hoped to set an example for construction elsewhere in the state. As much as possible, they wanted to preserve the landscape and use natural stone and wood for building materials. John Storrs, the Portland architect the Grays selected to design Salishan, explains that the idea was to have "a resort in repose. Salishan looks as if it dropped from the sky. It fits. It doesn't startle you." The weathered gray cedar main lodge connects, via covered walkways constructed of cedar and spruce, to a succession of smaller lodges housing the guest rooms. The sloping roofs and angular lines of the natural cedar buildings are modern, yet not boldly so. The colors mesh nicely with the hues of the evergreens, which rise to a prodigious height on this misty stretch of coast, and the soft gray-gold of the skies. (Brilliant sunny days do exist, but no one seems to mind the prevalent haze.)

Out in front of the lodge is a giant stump of Sitka spruce, one of many on the

The main lodge.

property. Years ago the local Salish Indians (from whom the lodge derives its name) used the Sitka's prickly boughs for bath brushes. During the World War I era, vast forests of Sitka spruce were cut down to provide wood for aircraft—among them, Howard Hughes's famous *Spruce Goose*. In Oregon the stumps are a point of pride, symbols of the state's contribution to the war effort as well as a reminder of how quickly nature can be destroyed. Near the stump is a clump of salal, another valued Oregon resource. The Indians used to dry the sour-tasting salal berries, form them into giant 15-pound cakes, then soak them in seal or whale oil in preparation for a feast. All over Salishan's grounds, native trees and plants flourish, and the management even provides a botanical guide in the rooms.

The lodge's interiors are studies in the successful merging of indoors and out. In the lobby, which is paneled with Western red cedar, a spray of fresh huckleberry leaves fills a vase on one side of the fireplace. The stones for the fireplace were carted from a local quarry. The lobby furniture, simple Scandinavian-style sofas and chairs, is upholstered in woodsy greens and browns. The nearby coffee shop is paneled in West Coast hemlock, and the Gourmet Dining Room in walnut. From virtually any seat in the vaulted, three-story dining room, one can gaze at the water through the vast expanse of window. Upstairs in the Attic Lounge, the chandeliers are made of "Japanese floats," those colored-glass balls Japanese fishermen have used for centuries on their nets. The floats, which are washed across the Pacific by the currents, were found on local beaches.

These natural elements provide a unique backdrop, as does another Salishan feature: the artwork. John and Betty Gray, longtime supporters of the Oregon art world, were determined to display the local product. "There was an attitude around here that art created outside the state had more value than what was made in Oregon," recalls Betty. "We wanted to help change that." Hence, in decorating Salishan, they purchased and commissioned all kinds of art from local craftsmen. The first piece to catch the visitor's eye is a delicate bird, sculpted from driftwood by Mark Sponenburg, a member of the art faculty at Oregon State University. Tucked into the foliage outside the front door, it rests on a stone pylon like a benign guardian.

Just inside the red-oak doors is a tree fashioned of weathered steel. Wandering through the main lodge, the guest finds bold abstracts of landscapes, as well as carvings and sculptures that are often an integral part of the decor. Artist Eugene Bennett's bas-relief sculpture forms the back wall of the Attic Lounge bar. The teak doors leading into a dining room called the Cedar Tree are carved by Roy Setziol, as are the 13 bas-relief teak panels in the nearby Gourmet Dining Room. For those interested in a more formal presentation of Oregon art, there are rotating exhibitions in the gallery. (Local artists often wait three years to participate in the shows.)

169

Guests appear to accept all this art as a part of Salishan. A low-key bunch, they wander through the lobby in their golf and tennis clothes and head down the hillside with their binoculars to look for birds in the estuary. On the sandspit dense with beach grass, they prowl up and down the shore examining hunks of driftwood washed up by the Oregon storms. In fact, a few of the regulars relish putting on a sou'wester and boots and walking the beach buffeted by the rain and winds. These veteran storm watchers leave a standing order with the management: "Call us if you see a really good one rolling in!" (Generally, the big shows are in winter.)

For less intrepid guests, a really good day at Salishan might mean nothing more than a saunter to man-made Lake Salishan, where nutria and muskrat swim in the waters. Or it could mean a game of golf on a course that meanders up the hillside and down onto the sandspit. A bald eagle or a great blue heron just might soar overhead as golfers line up their shots.

In the late afternoon, around nap time, there is a soft knock at the door. "Fresh kindling," says the young man who has arrived to make sure the stack by the fireplace is as it should be. Later it's time for a few drinks in the Attic Lounge, followed by dinner. "There's no social director around here, no breezy-voiced woman organizing bridge or canasta in the evenings," warns a staffer. "We don't want that." Most of the guests prefer a leisurely candlelight dinner, which often includes Chinook salmon caught in the waters nearby.

The Chinook has a special significance in these parts. Years ago, when coastal Oregon was the preserve of the Salish Indians, salmon was the principal food source. Salmon, accompanied by cattail roots, huckleberries, and salal, was also the main dish at an elaborate ritual known as a potlatch. This was an early expression of socialism in which an Indian who had amassed riches (such as red-headed woodpecker capes) invited his tribesmen to a big party. During the festivities, he gave away his worldy goods. No sooner had he done so than he started acquiring *new* wealth. Meanwhile, the recipients of his largess gave their *own* potlatches. The cycle continued. At these gatherings, the Salish, dressed in cedar bark and bearskins, danced around the Chinook as it roasted over an open pit.

Today, salmon still reigns in the Northwest. At Salishan it is served not only in the dining rooms but at periodic salmon bakes on one of the outdoor patios. As guests mill about nibbling pâté and sole mousse, the flames from a giant brazier send out a red-gold light against the dark sky. A chef in a white toque emerges from the kitchen with hefty filets of Chinook. Using willow twigs, he lashes them to planks made of alder wood and sets them over the coals. Selections from maître d'hotel Phil DeVito's wine cellar flow.

Such pleasures in the woods have not gone unnoticed. Salishan is no longer Oregon's best-kept secret. The guest roster, heavily Northwestern in the sixties when the Grays opened their resort, now has its share of visitors from all over the United States, even Hollywood. Actor Ed Asner liked the area so much that

Salishan Lodge

A sandspit across from the lodge.

he bought a home nearby. Shirley MacLaine loves the salmon fishing. Oregon's former governor, the late Tom McCall, was practically part of the family. During his tenure he made Salishan a favorite spot for high-level meetings. Increasingly, other Northwest leaders are scheduling conferences at the lodge.

Ironically, when the Grays first began purchasing what eventually became a 700-acre spread, they weren't thinking about a hotel. The plan was to construct a community of vacation homes on the sandspit and up the hill. "We had found coming down here to the beach a way of recharging our lives," recalls Betty. "We wanted to develop a place where creative people could come and get recharged as we did." A small "mom-and-pop inn" on the grounds, they thought, might be nice. "Then I got a little more expansive in my ideas," recalls John. As construction on the homesites proceeded, so did increasingly grand plans for a lodge. Gray and architect Storrs spent days driving around the hillside site in a jeep. They stopped to put up marking string wherever they especially liked the views.

Two decades later, Gray is pleased with his decision. Besides proving that a resort can be both conservation-minded and commercial, he has gained immense personal satisfaction. "I'm not a craftsman," he says. "And I can't paint or sketch. With Salishan, I feel like I've painted on the landscape. It's my way of creating."

Gleneden Beach, Oregon   97388

Telephone
503-764-2371

On the Premises: The lodge has 151 rooms, which overlook either the water or the golf course. The course itself is an 18-hole, par-72 links course. Salishan also has three indoor tennis courts and one outdoor, hard-surface court, a 20 × 60-foot indoor swimming pool with separate whirlpool tub and adjacent gym and saunas, and jogging and hiking trails. A special token available at the front desk provides access to Salishan's beach. The icy waters, strong currents, and crashing waves are to be seriously heeded; swimmers should stick to the pool. Fishermen will find that this is superb salmon country.

Rooms: Salishan's wood-paneled accommodations are spacious and modern. Functional rather than lavish, they are furnished with comfortable club chairs and reading lights, unobtrusive print and woven fabrics, and color TVs. The fireplaces are built into the walls at waist level, perhaps to avoid all that bending over to stoke the wood. In the baths, the vanities have two basins and plenty of space to spread out makeup and shaving equipment; there are stacks of fresh towels, bath gel, and a collapsible clothesline in the tub (even a little container of detergent for hand washing). Laundry service is, of course, available.

Meals: Breakfast is served in the coffee shop. Omelets filled with salmon or Dungeness crab are on the menu, along with ouefs en cocotte, hazelnut pancakes, fruit cobbler, and blueberry crumb cake. At lunchtime, one can order salads and sandwiches or heartier entrees such as oyster stew and curried shrimp. In the evening, guests have their choice of the candlelit Gourmet Dining Room or the more casual Cedar Tree (which is closed during the

quiet winter months). In the Gourmet Dining Room, the local delicacies include smoked Pacific trout, Petrale sole topped with Oregon filberts, and, of course, Chinook salmon; Continental dishes such as chateaubriand with morel sauce and rack of lamb are available too.

Getting There: Some businessmen arrive by private corporate jet at the adjacent landing strip. Most guests land in Portland, 90 miles northeast of Salishan. Salishan is located on Highway 101 between Lincoln City and Depoe Bay.

Money Matters: Salishan operates on the European plan. A double ranges from $68 to $88; larger rooms called chieftains (a wooden louvered screen separates the sleeping and sitting areas) range from $86 to $110; the three suites vary from $200 to $282. Salishan accepts MasterCard, Visa, American Express, and Diners Club.

Side Trips: A trained Audubon Society lecturer is available for guided trail walks. A few miles south of the lodge in Depoe Bay, which bills itself as "the world's smallest harbor," charter and sightseeing boats stand by. In winter and spring, the boats are a good place to watch the parade of gray whales passing along the Oregon coast on their annual migration from the Arctic waters to the lagoons of Mexico.

Observations: Don't forget that the weather in coastal Oregon can be cool and capricious, which is part of the appeal. Summer, always temperate, comes about two months late, and is an especially popular time for travelers eager to escape areas of sticky heat. Nor

The Sunset Suite.

should you come here expecting velvets, antiques, and other traditional trappings of elegance. The furnishings are casual, even modest. The setting, the emphasis on ecology (they ask you to recycle the brochures), the artwork, and the sports are the appeal. Also keep in mind that a highway (there is an underpass, once used for cattle) and sandspit separate Salishan from the water; plans to build Salishan right on the sandspit were rejected as a way of preserving the ecology of the fragile waterfront land and the privacy of the homeowners on the spit.

23 *Rosario Resort*

Eastsound, Orcas Island, Washington

I sland hopping is one of those questing pleasures in life one associates with the Caribbean or the Aegean. But in the far reaches of the Pacific Northwest, a group of 172 islands stretches, like stepping-stones, from the mainland of Washington to Vancouver Island and Canada. The San Juans—the nation's largest island chain—dot northern Puget Sound and challenge any explorer. Some of this rocky real estate is inhabited, some not. The navigator can easily drop anchor at a small fishing village one day and at a deserted, driftwood-strewn beach the next.

The sunny San Juans, as they are called, are a fluke of nature. The cold winds and rain that all too often darken the Washington coast generally bypass the islands. At worst, in the late autumn and winter, a mist seeps over the San Juans, transforming the terrain into a surreal haze of land and sea. Overhead, bald eagles ride the wind currents, swerving off and disappearing into the fog surrounding the pine forests.

The largest of the islands, and a good place to pull into port, is Orcas Island. This is considered by many to be the choicest salmon-fishing grounds in the nation. Salmon run along three sides of the horseshoe-shaped, 56-square-mile island. Orcas is also the home of Rosario Resort, a historic old hotel that caters to islomaniacs. These are people who, as Lawrence Durrell wrote in *Reflections on a Marine Venus*, "find islands somehow irresistible. The mere knowledge that they are on an island, a little world surrounded by the sea, fills them with an indescribable intoxication."

For those afflicted with islomania, the intoxicated feeling begins en route. The most common approach to Rosario is via the Washington State Ferry, a triple-decker vehicle that can hold up to 200 cars and 500 people. As the ferry chugs out of Anacortes, a town two hours north of Seattle, it picks up speed and weaves through the channels of the San Juans. The snowcapped peaks of the northern Cascade Mountain Range are silhouettes in the distance. The fin of an *Orcinas Orca* (killer whale) pokes above the water as the passengers rush to the deck. "Look! Jaws II!" shouts a young boy. His parents, who seem to have been this route before, explain to him that the killer whales, despite their name, are not partial to humans.

Ninety minutes later, the boat docks at Eastbound on Orcas Island. Then comes a half-hour car ride through a nineteenth-century landscape of unfenced meadows where horses roam and deer scamper. Suddenly, there is civilization. Smoke puffs from the 10 chimneys of a white-gabled mansion at the edge of the water. Its scores of windows glimmer like portholes on an ocean liner. On the lawn, a pine figurehead of a woman, carved in 1874 and salvaged from the wreck of the clipper *America* in 1915, looks out to sea.

Rosario was constructed by a Seattle shipbuilder, Robert Moran, and his nautical influences are everywhere. The multicolored flags of seven nations — Japan, Great Britain, Canada, Sweden, Germany, Austria, and the United States — flutter from the balcony, almost as if the hotel were an international marina. Inside the lobby, shiny brass railings and couplings on doors and windows are like those in an elegant stateroom. The windows, made of seaworthy seven-eighths-inch glass, swing open sideways on thick brass hinges. The mahogany walls and benches might be the outfitting of a captain's cabin. Upstairs in the three-story mansion, the hallways are lined with framed photographs of the USS *Nebraska*, which Moran built for the U.S. government in 1904.

Many of the guests who visit this island resort are also boat lovers. If they don't arrive by ferry, they are likely to cruise into Rosario's private marina, where they might even sleep on board their yachts. Were it not for the shadow of the Cascades in the distance, the harbor could be almost anywhere, from Nantucket to Newport Beach. The marina itself is one of those typically friendly communities where people sit in deck chairs on their power boats and sip Scotch, nodding to the passersby. Most come from the Pacific Northwest, but a few are members of the international set one finds in Mykonos or Portofino. A woman chattering animatedly in Italian to her husband grabs her tennis racket and heads off to Rosario's courts. A French couple wearing matching white jeans and T-shirts return to their 40-foot sailboat with a bag of ice.

Many of the skippers prefer the landlubbing diversions of Rosario. After days at sea, they like the feeling of sleeping in a brass bed in one of the rooms in the old mansion, or perhaps in a more modern suite in a separate waterfront villa. They like wandering beneath the madrona trees and tall pines that frame the old mansion, soaking in the sauna, or hunting for driftwood on the beach. Their kids are soon landlocked in the Fun Zone, which is equipped with billiard tables, pinball machines, and video games.

In the late afternoon, vacationers might converge in the Music Room on the second floor. The 1,972 pipes of the Aeolian organ are built into the walls or housed in two large cases on either side of the room. The light coming through the stained-glass windows, imported from Belgium and depicting the harbor at Antwerp, casts an amber glow on the pipes and the expanse of wood-paneled walls. Guests dressed in sneakers, shorts, and golf pants settle down in leather club chairs. They listen as a tuxedoed young man named Christopher Peacock give a 45-minute organ recital.

The resort's creator used to play this organ (rather badly, it is said) at 7 A.M. to awaken guests he had invited to his island hideaway. Robert Moran was a strong-minded sort who believed the world should operate on his terms. Even as a young man, he showed a determined streak. As Glenn and Mildred Carlson, Orcas Island historians, recount in *The Rosario Story*, Moran left his New York City home at age seventeen. The son of a machinist, he set out walking in 1874. Eventually, after a few setbacks, Moran got to the Northwest. As a deckhand and later a fireman on steamers and stern-wheelers, he traveled to Alaska. In 1882, with $1,600 in capital, he opened a marine repair shop on Yesler Wharf in Seattle. By 1889, at thirty-two years of age, Moran was one of the most prosperous businessmen in the area — and mayor of Seattle. Then came the terrible Seattle fire that wiped out most of the town. Undaunted, Moran started over with a shipbuilding and repair company that was soon building the flat-bottom, shallow-draft and stern-wheelers ideal for carrying food and supplies to the Alaskan goldfields.

Then, in 1904, Moran developed a heart problem. His doctors told him he had only six months to live. Determined to spend his last days in a perfect island hideaway, Moran began buying up land on Orcas. He selected a site on a rocky bluff overlooking Cascade Bay and built his mansion. The local loggers and fishermen had never seen anything like it. Even Moran's Seattle friends who came to visit were impressed, not only with the property but with their host's noticeably improved health. The women unpacked their long dresses and Paris hats in the teak closets; the men hung up their tuxedos. They strolled the grounds in full dress, picnicked on the grass, played lawn games, and went boating in the bay.

177

The Music Room with its 1,972 pipe organ.

Moran played genial host. At other moments, he fished for salmon or wandered about with his camera. An early experimenter in color photography, he took thousands of pictures of the local islands and mountains (many of which have since been printed, framed, and hung throughout the mansion). Months, then years, passed, and Moran's health grew stronger. In 1939, at age eighty-two, he reflected back on the turn-of-the century pronouncement that he had half a year to live: "Thirty-five years ago, the medical profession was not as well informed on heart disease as it is today. My real trouble was a highly nervous condition brought on by a badly overworked physical and mental life. This condition affected the heart's action and deceived the doctors, as is proved now when the old pump seems to be giving perfect hydraulic service."

After the death of his wife that year, Moran decided to sell Rosario (named after a nearby strait) to Donald Rheem, a California industrialist. He moved to a quiet spot a mile or so down the sound, where he lived until his death in 1943. Under the proprietorship of the Rheems family, the old mansion grew even more opulent. The family spent hundreds of thousands on Oriental rugs and antiques; they installed a motion-picture projection room on an interior balcony in the Music Room. On the front lawn, they built a bandstand so that they could greet arriving guests with a musical flourish. It wasn't until 1960, a few years after the Rheems had sold the property, that the gracious estate became a resort. The new owners, Gil and Glee Geiser of Seattle, greatly expanded Rosario, building suites, guest rooms, and boat moorings. In 1980 the Geisers sold the resort to a trio of local businessmen, Manfred Cieslik, Gerdta Foust, and Jim Roberts, who have continued to renovate and restore.

Today, Rosario is a far livelier place than it was in the days when Moran took solitary walks through the evergreens and fished for salmon off the rocks. Deer still venture onto the grounds, but are sometimes frightened away by a jogger. The lawn bordering the seawall is now dotted with sunbathers and children playing Frisbee.

One of the most exciting times to be at Rosario is December, when the resort schedules its annual two-day Salmon Derby. First prize, $10,000, goes to the fisherman who pulls in the biggest salmon (the record is 17 pounds, 5 ounces). In 1981, in a spirit of liberation, the management added a special prize for the biggest salmon caught by a woman (a 12-pounder is the record).

Robert Moran, a product of the Victorian era, may or may not have approved of this gesture. But one thing seems certain. The pioneering shipbuilder would be pleased to sit on the pillared porch of the mansion he built and watch the salmon fleet. Like many inhabitants of the Pacific Northwest, he was of the belief that goin' salmon fishing is one of the best ways to solve life's problems.

Rosario Resort

Eastsound, Orcas Island,
Washington   98245

Telephone
206-376-2222

On the Premises: Rosario is a community consisting of an old mansion, various outer buildings, and a marina with 45 moorings and 30 buoys. Guests arriving by boat can stay on board or at the resort, where there are three swimming pools, six hard-surface tennis courts, horseback riding, a narrow, 2-mile beach, and golf available at a nearby nine-hole course. The fishing for sea bass, rock cod, ling cod, red snapper, and salmon is excellent, and charter boats are available. For a quiet afternoon, the library contains the original owner's collection of 10,000 books, ranging from a 1901 Rand McNally Atlas to a mint-condition collection of Zane Grey's works.

Rooms: The 215 accommodations at Rosario vary widely. The most picturesque are the rooms in the old mansion that are furnished with brass beds, down quilts, and overstuffed wing chairs. Teak and mahogany frame the doors and windows; the light comes from

wall lamps, circa 1930. The villas overlooking the water have spectacular views and an English country-house elegance (wing chairs, brass lamps, floral-print bedspreads). The modern haciendas, separate condominium-style buildings on a hillside, can be rented as one-, two-, or three-bedroom accommodations. There is also a "boatel" by the dock with rooms that are simply furnished.

Meals: The day usually begins for Rosario guests with a big breakfast. Blueberry pancakes and waffles with fresh strawberries and whipped cream are on the menu, along with corned-beef hash and eggs Benedict. Lunches consist of salads, burgers, and sandwiches. At dinner, the Continental menu offers the local fresh-shucked oysters and Pacific salmon, as well as specialties like veal topped with Dungeness crab and asparagus spears, and calf's sweetbread meunière.

Getting There: Unless one arrives by private boat, the most common approach to Orcas Island is by the Washington State Ferry, which leaves from either Anacortes in Washington, or from Sidney, British Columbia. (The hotel will send schedules on request.) For those who want a shorter, if less scenic, trip, San Juan Airlines flies to Eastsound Airport from Seattle-Tacoma International Airport. The resort's van will pick up passengers at the ferry dock or airport on request.

Money Matters: Rosario operates on the European plan, with deluxe doubles priced at $77 per night; suites range from $125 to $145. The resort accepts MasterCard, Visa, American Express, and Diners Club.

Side Trips: Eastsound, the principal town on the island, has a little English church, clapboard houses, and antiques and pottery shops where prices are still within reason. The Orcas Island Historical Museum, located in the heart of Eastsound, has a collection of Indian artifacts (kept in a fireproof vault), old sewing machines, spinning wheels, a dentist's drill with foot pedal, and the old Eastsound Post Office front. In Moran State Park, a 5,000-acre preserve donated by Rosario's founder, Robert Moran, hikers can climb to the summit of Mount Constitution for a panoramic view of the islands and the Cascade Mountains.

Observations: This is a remote, romantic place for those who appreciate a sense of isolation. Come expecting an island pace, good sporting facilities, and a relatively quiet experience. Remember that unless you come by private boat, the ferry—which does not take reservations—is the main way on or off. If you get cabin fever, Rosario may not be the resort for you.

180

Rosario Resort

24 *Kapalua Bay Hotel*

Kapalua, Maui, Hawaii

Long ago, when Maui's palm-fringed beaches were largely deserted stretches of sand, the humpback whale, an exuberant 40-ton leviathan, journeyed to these warm waters

each winter to play and mate. Inevitably, Maui's most faithful visitor was joined by another class of mammal: the tourist. In the early 1960s, the *malihinis* (literally "strangers" in Hawaiian) discovered the humpback's bedroom waters. They soon staged a massive invasion on Sunfishes, catamarans, power boats, and surfboards. Today, proclaiming Maui the last paradise, they rave about its volcano Haleakala, its lush subtropical rain forests, its brooding mountains and bleached beaches. The island's illicit and, reportedly, unsurpassable marijuana crop gets special mention and is nicknamed Maui Wowie.

With the onslaught has come the inevitable signs of trouble in paradise. The locals joke that the state bird is the airplane (it's the nene) and fret that the land taxes are going up as fast as the high-rises and condominiums. Indeed, an epidemic of condo fever is sweeping areas of coastal Maui. Clusters of towering, Miami Beach–style hotels hug the shore.

For adventurous tourists, the first view of Maui might be from one of the nine-passenger Cessnas operated by Royal Hawaiian Air Service. Regular jets do land on the island, but they don't offer the special services of Royal Hawaiian. The pilots, after weighing not only the luggage but the passengers to make sure the load is right, often provide a running commentary en route. On the half-hour hop from Honolulu, a passenger might learn all about Hawaii's weather patterns. He will get, literally, a bird's-eye view of Diamond Head, and the opportunity to photograph the tumbling waterfalls and jagged cliffs of Molokai from a very comfortable distance. He will also be shown Father Damien's famous leper colony on a deserted Molokai shore. As the little gold plane noses down on the runway at Maui's Kaanapali Airport, the passenger may have another surprise: clouds of smoke billowing from the nearby fields. "Don't be alarmed folks," the pilot will probably say. "It's just the farmers burning the leaves off the sugarcane."

At the airport, a driver will likely be waiting for those passengers staying at the Kapalua Bay Hotel. Within 20 minutes they will arrive at a resort that is a few miles and a psychological ocean removed from the discos, nightclubs, and tourist groups of the Maui high-rises. The man behind it, a fifth-generation Maui islander, was determined to build a hotel that would be a model for proper development in the entire state. The specter of overdeveloped Waikiki was sobering. "What we wanted at Kapalua," says its founder, businessman

182

Kapalua Bay
Hotel

and planter Colin Cameron, "was a building that would not quarrel with the landscape. This is an island, a rural place. To be driving along the road and suddenly to be hit with a 10-story building is obscene."

Kapalua is a graceful six-story terraced structure that slopes down to two stories at sea level. Standing by its circular driveway landscaped with Chinese banyans and perfumed Singapore plumeria, one sees an angular, sandy-colored building. Free-standing concrete pillars crisscross with beams at the top to form a dramatic open portico. Louvered shutters angle outward to let in the breezes from the mountains on one side and the sea on the other.

Inside the multi-storied lobby, one is suddenly in a tropical rain forest that has been tamed and accessorized by a decorator. A profusion of pothos plants hangs from the ceiling in pots; the leaves of fan, fishtail, and areca palms rustle. A waterfall tumbles down a wall. A fountain and a pool, straddled by a footbridge, separate the two sides of the dining room on the lower level. In the shallow waters shine quarters, drachmas, pesos, francs, and other coins tossed in by an international parade of visitors. Red ti leaves (the green ones are used for hula skirts and also to wrap the pig at a luau) ring the fountain. Against this botanical backdrop, the rattan couches and peacock chairs upholstered in muted, batiklike island prints look suitably tropical. The lacquered Oriental chairs and end tables pay homage to Hawaii's rich Asian heritage.

Kapalua guests have their choice of staying in the 194-room hotel or in one of the privately owned condominiums, many of which are available for rental. The actress Carol Burnett was so charmed by the sleek, faintly Japanese-style condos that she bought three. Tim Conway and Vicki Lawrence have also purchased property at Kapalua. This small contingent of movie stars lives in complexes behind locked gates, but does show up at the hotel's restaurants now and then, especially when entertaining visiting Hollywood friends.

For the movie stars and regular guests alike, one of Kapalua's special appeals is its tranquil ambience. There is always a quiet corner for reading in the lobby and a seat in the dining rooms. The regulars, often hard-working professional couples and families who return as often as possible, appreciate the fact that there are no noisy bands or glitzy, overdressed crowds. They like being able to pick up the ingredients for a picnic lunch in the gourmet deli (you can even *eat* there if you don't feel like a full-course dinner). They welcome the little touches, such as the umbrella in the closet in case there is a sudden tropical storm, the floral arrangements everywhere (even in the baths), and the orchids presented to the ladies when they leave the Veranda Dining Room. Again and again, they remark about the unusual friendliness of the staff.

First stop for many guests is one of the two golf courses, where silvery green pineapple fields border some of the fairways. Other visitors tuck away suitcases that originated in New York, Texas, California, England, or perhaps Japan, and head straight for the beach. The adults settle down on the eggshell white sand and gaze at the islands of Molokai and Lanai in the distance. Kids paddle back and forth on yellow rafts. The more athletic visitors attend the wind-surfing demonstrations on Wednesday and Saturday or go out sailing and

184

**Kapalua
Bay Hotel**

snorkeling on a catamaran. The snorkeling, most agree, is excellent. The kaleidoscopic *uhu* (parrot fish), striped *manini* (surgeon fish), and spindly reddish purple lionfish swim by yellow and white coral and an occasional ruin of a car that tumbled into the bay from a cliff.

After a day at the beach, guests might find a small orchestra playing Liszt and Debussey in the lobby. (This is the Kapalua Music Assembly, which the management helped create to teach violin and piano to the West Maui children and to give music performances.) Or, Kapalua guests might attend the regular classes in lei making, palm-frond weaving, and quilt making that are designed to give visitors an introduction to island crafts. Over at the botanical garden, the hotel displays plants indigenous to the Hawaiian islands. Up in the hills near one of the two golf courses, the remnants of an old plantation village will be restored for the enjoyment of local residents as well as hotel guests. There are also plans for archaeological tours of the early Hawaiian temple sites on the property.

All this reflects the management's belief that Hawaii's heritage should be preserved and made accessible to interested guests. The man behind the policy is owner Cameron, whose great-great-grandfather, the Reverend Dwight Baldwin, was a doctor and Hawaiian missionary. Baldwin came to the islands in 1830 from Durham, Connecticut. He settled in Lahaina, then Maui's brawling whaling port. (Baldwin's home, constructed of coral, stone, and hand-hewn timbers, has been restored and turned into a museum.) The reverend's son, Henry Perrine Baldwin, later helped found Alexander & Baldwin, one of Hawaii's major sugarcane, shipping, and development companies. Around the turn of the century, H. P. Baldwin acquired the Honolua Ranch, site of the present-day

Kapalua Bay Hotel. In the early days, Angus cattle grazed on the ranch; watermelon, mango, papaya, litchi, and avocado were grown on its volcanic slopes.

Gradually, pineapple became an important crop, thanks to the efforts of Colin Cameron's father, a Boston advertising man who had married into the Baldwin family. (Colin himself returned to Boston to attend Harvard Business School before entering the family business.) By the early 1960s, Cameron began to feel that it was time to diversify. "Pineapple had its up and downs," he explains. "I felt we needed something else, and tourism seemed to be the wave of the future." Eventually the Kapalua Land Company, a subsidiary of Maui Land & Pineapple Company, of which Cameron is chairman, was formed. In 1978 the neophyte developer opened his resort and hired Rockresorts to manage it. The management was later assumed by Regent International Hotels, which runs it today.

For its logo, the hotel created a butterfly with a pineapple in the center, a symbol of the metamorphosis from pineapple field to resort. At Kapalua the little butterfly is almost as ubiquitous as the Izod reptile. It appears on the shorts, shirts, tote bags, umbrellas, sun hats, even golf bags the guests buy in the special Logo Shop in the hotel's boutique area. They also purchase the Burmese jade, Maui pink coral, Indonesian batiks, Imari bronzes, and shell leis sold in Kapalua's various shops, said to be the best on the island.

By the time they are ready to leave Kapalua, most guests have acquired a suitcase full of gifts, a deep honey-gold tan, and possibly a better golf score or backhand. Most will readily agree with the local saying, widely displayed on island T-shirts: MAUI NO KA OI ("MAUI IS THE BEST").

**Kapalua
Bay Hotel**

One Bay Drive
Kapalua, Maui, Hawaii   96761

Telephone
808-669-5656

On the Premises: Kapalua operates a little like a cruise ship at sea. It offers visitors a full schedule of classes in calisthenics, crafts, Japanese flower arranging, even feeding of tropical fish, as well as evening lectures on Hawaii's history and landscape. The hotel has two 18-hole championship golf courses, one of which was designed by Arnold Palmer, and 10 hard-surface tennis courts. There is a large zigzag pool as well as a lovely beach. Sailing, surfing, scuba diving, snorkeling, and deep-sea fishing can be arranged for in the beach area.

Rooms: Spacious and tastefully furnished in subtle island print fabrics and rattan, the accommodations at Kapalua are especially nice.

An overhead fan twirls for those who don't want to turn on the air conditioning. A refrigerator is tucked away in a built-in console. The lanai faces the ocean or the mountains. The baths are all quite large and outfitted with his and her vanities, a big closet for him (man-size slippers and umbrella are inside) and a big closet for her (she gets a scale), and separate tub and shower stall.

Meals: Kapalua has three restaurants, the main dining room, the Bay Club, which is directly on the water, and the Plantation Veranda, designed to look like a turn-of-the-century Hawaiian plantation manor house. Breakfast is served in the main dining room

187

and begins with steaming Kona coffee. Guava or passion-fruit juice might be followed by orange pancakes garnished with flowers, waffles with fresh coconut syrup, broiled local fish, or eggs. The pastries are tempting: macadamia nut Danish, freshly baked banana bread, and sticky pecan rolls. At lunchtime most guests try the massive buffet in the main dining room. Steamed *mahimahi* (native dolphinfish), lemon chicken, or black-bean duck might be the hot dishes of the day accompanied by endless salads and Molokai bread (like sourdough). At dinnertime, guests can select from a sophisticated international menu in the Plantation Veranda, Bay Club, or main dining room. (The latter two also offer a table d'hôte menu featuring the cuisine of a foreign land.) In the Veranda, perhaps the most gourmet of the three, delicacies include smoked eel, ring-necked pheasant pâté, and a quenelles soufflé, accompanied by a superb selection of California-only wines. European wines are served in the other dining rooms.

Getting There: The island's major airport at Kahului is serviced by regular commuter jets. The closest airport is at Kaanapali, where Royal Hawaiian lands its Cessnas. From either airport, take Route 30 to the hotel.

Money Matters: Kapalua's 194 rooms range in price from $143 to $183 per day, European plan. The three suites cost about $350. The hotel accepts MasterCard, Visa, American Express, and Diners Club.

Side Trips: Maui, the so-called Valley Isle, is verdant and widely varying. Hana, an authentic Hawaiian village on the eastern tip of the island, is surrounded by dense rain forest; Lahaina, a picturesque whaling port on the west coast, bakes in almost relentless sun. Both are worth a visit. The volcano Haleakala, at the center of a 28,000-acre national park, is a must and can be ascended by car or horse.

Observations: Kapalua's position on a windswept hillside isolated from the tourist crush has pluses and minuses. This spot is secluded but also prone to more wind and rain than other places on the West Maui Coast. However, the winds can be a blessing on a hot day. Also, if the rains persist, there probably will be a sunny beach a few miles away. Hawaiian weather varies dramatically from one spot to the next.

188

**Kapalua
Bay Hotel**

25 *Mauna Kea Beach Hotel*

Kamuela, Hawaii

**Mauna Kea
Beach Hotel**

T he Big Island, as the locals call Hawaii, is famous for its orchids, coffee, macadamia nuts,
and a history as glorious — and at times as
blood red — as the sunsets over its volcanic

peaks. This, the largest island in the chain, is the birthplace of Kamehameha I,
the great warrior king who unified the archipelago in the late eighteenth century and established the foundations of the modern Hawaiian state. It is also
the place where Captain Cook, the discoverer of the islands, was stabbed to
death and stripped of his flesh by the natives in 1779.

In subsequent years the missionaries came to the island, along with the cattle
ranchers, *paniolos* (cowboys decked out in blue denim shirts, bandanas, and
straw hats), farmers, and land developers. Yet, the Big Island has somehow
managed to avoid the boom of overdevelopment that has transformed parts of
Oahu from a tropical jungle into an urban one. The island of Hawaii, with its
4,003 square miles, still has only about 92,000 people and manages to retain an
ambience of isolated serenity. It has deserted, exotic black-sand beaches and a
few the color of French-vanilla ice cream. It has a dramatic terrain that shifts
from lush forests to moonscapelike lava fields (the result of recent eruptions of
its still-active volcanoes). It also has the most consistent weather on the islands,
thanks to the brooding hulks of Mauna Kea and its sister volcano, Mauna Loa,
which keep the rain clouds away until afternoon. Naturally, Hawaii suffers
certain encroachments of civilization. Madame Pele, the Hawaiian fire goddess
who haunts the craters of Hawaii Volcanoes National Park, used to demand a
sprig of local ohelo berries as an offering. These days, she is apparently just as
happy with the little airline bottles of gin left for her on the fire pit of the main
crater.

If goddesses can compromise, so can the locals. The islanders lament the
inevitable passing of a simpler way of life. In the small towns, a few old-timers
believe stripped ti leaves ward off evil spirits and honor individual family gods,
such as whales, sharks, and eels. Most of the residents, however, welcome the
expansion of industry — especially tourism — as a way of keeping pace with the
growth of the 50th state.

The hotel that put the Big Island on the "must see" list kept by the world's
discriminating islomaniacs is the Mauna Kea. Literally chiseled out of a lava
field, it stands alone in man-made verdure on the island's most perfect, cres-
cent-shaped beach. The creator, the conservation-minded Laurance S. Rockefeller, had been asked in 1960 to help the Hawaiian government develop tourist
areas to stimulate the new state's economy. "Almost immediately, I was struck

by the beauty of the area where the slope of Mauna Kea mountain levels down to that magnificent curved beach," Rockefeller remembers of the day he first surveyed the site where he would eventually build his resort. "The area was a wilderness, almost a desert, and the idea of building a hotel there with a golf course was a terrific challenge."

Driving toward the Mauna Kea, surveying the dark fields of lava and the arid cattle land bristling with cacti, the visitor can easily understand the enormity of Rockefeller's challenge. But as one approaches the hotel, suddenly the grass turns as green as a banana leaf. (More than 1 million gallons of water a day are used to keep the lawns lush.) Bougainvillea and plumeria, their blossoms highlighting the landscape, scent the air. Turning into the Mauna Kea's circular driveway, the arriving guest views a sleek, rather rectagonal structure that hugs the lava bluff. From a distance, especially in the light of evening, it looks a little like an ocean liner adrift at sea. But up close, it is a study in modern design concepts. The architects, Skidmore, Owings, & Merrill, believed in exposing natural materials (the pattern of the construction forms is still apparent in the concrete).

As a guest enters the lobby, the first surprise is the sight of two bronze Buddhas (actually, you will learn later by reading the hotel's literature that they are seated *disciples* of Buddha). The next is the pretty young woman in a slinky island print dress who greets you with "Aloha! Welcome to the Mauna Kea." Later, after you have gaped at the 60-foot palms (dropped in by crane and denuded of coconuts to avoid hitting anyone on the head) in the central courtyard, you will be escorted to your room by this same young woman. She will lead you, perhaps, past the twisting Japanese garden where brightly colored koi

**Mauna Kea
Beach Hotel**

fish swim in the pools, and past walls covered with exotically patterned quilts and bark-cloth tapestries (more about this later). In your room, she will gesture toward the lanai, a patio that faces either the mountains or the sea, and point out the Japanese summer kimonos (*yukatas*) laid out neatly on the bed. A little card notes that they are for use during your stay, and that the management will gladly launder them on request (the Mauna Kea employs a full-time *yukata* presser). Your hostess might also note the ice bucket hidden discreetly in a red lacquer Oriental chest, and the refrigerator tucked under the marble vanity in the bath. You quickly get the impression that anything the least unsightly at the Mauna Kea is concealed. Refusing a tip, the hostess slips away.

Poking around on your own, you will see the delicate hand of a discriminating millionaire. Even though Laurance Rockefeller sold the Mauna Kea to Westin Hotels in 1978, many of the little touches he insisted upon remain. The soap, for example, is a big, 1½-ounce bar of Yardley because Rockefeller hated those little hotel slivers that slip out of your hands and down the drain. The bed linens are 100 percent cotton. The pretty pottery coffee mugs in the bath are meant to hold toothbrushes.

Of all the Mauna Kea touches, nothing dazzles like the art. It is everywhere you look, from the valuable Hawaiian quilts and bark cloth on the walls, to the Chinese bronze drums and Indian brass storage chests (*chamlas*) that serve as occasional pieces in the lobby. The collection, more than 1,000 pieces, was put together by Laurance Rockefeller to serve as the nucleus of the hotel's interior design. "These pieces reflect the hotel's Pacific character," he explains. "They draw upon primitive art, the oceanic and folk arts, and the enduring art of the ancient people of the Pacific areas. Hawaiian quilts were part of this Pacific heritage. The patterns of the quilts told a story of Hawaii's fruits, flowers, leaves, marine life, landmarks, and legends. So we commissioned a group of the islands' most talented quilt makers to create the Mauna Kea quilts. We sought to involve the Hawaiian culture and people as much as possible."

This thoughtful collection is incorporated into the hotel landscape. A seventeenth-century Indian Buddha, perhaps the most valuable piece in the collection, is situated not far from a shuffleboard court. In one of the dining rooms, a Hawaiian calabash with a sculptured edge used to wipe poi (pounded taro root) from the fingers rests near a silver tray piled high with macadamia nut after-dinner candies. At the south end of the elevator lobby, near the entrance to the bar, is part of a primitive New Guinea carved house post, the badge of the clan. Virtually everywhere one looks, from the restaurants to the gardens, there is a priceless something: a Thai dragon, a Ceylonese phoenix, a Maori carved lintel, Cambodian temple bells and wind chimes, even a wall of tiny bronze Indian temple toys.

A guest room with its lanai.

Mauna Kea guests seem to accept this dramatic collection with equanimity. They attend the weekly art tours conducted by a hotel staffer, and walk around with the printed guide to the collection supplied in their rooms. Mostly, however, they regard the art as a backdrop. Like the sun, which shines practically every day of the year on this favored patch of island coast, it is a Mauna Kea given.

For those who order breakfast in their rooms, the day begins with a discreet knock. There is no rumble or clanking of breakfast cart preceding the knock. Rockefeller himself supposedly selected the noiseless wagons (they cost about $1,000 each), which have special shock absorbers to deaden the sound of the wheels. A waiter sets the table on the lanai with yellow and white linens, crystal, and fresh flowers and leaves a little toaster so that guests can pop in their own.

After breakfast the guests head out to the sun. In the elevators and cool, tile-floored lobbies, there are no scruffy jeans or holey tennis sneakers to be seen. At least not often. Slacks are silk and beautifully cut on the women, white or just possibly pastel on the men. The shorts are likely Frank Shorter, the sports shirts Izod, and the sweaters knotted over shoulders Polo. The heels of Gucci loafers (sans socks) click back and forth across the tiles. Outside the sundry shop on the lower lobby, which does a brisk early-morning business,

Alexander the parrot takes it all in from the interior of his large white Tunisian bird cage.

As the day progresses, the crowd disperses to the Bermuda grass of the golf course where, they'll tell you, each hole has its unique challenges. "Most courses are like welfare. You subsidize the poor player. Well, that's not true here," says an assistant golf pro. Over at the tennis courts, they provide smiling hostesses and clocks that are set on "Hawaiian time" (10 minutes slow).

It's down at the beach, however, that Mauna Kea truly shines. Bronzed, bikini-clad bodies stretch out on chaises under clumps of palms. Two Eastern lawyers who met the evening before over mai tais and macadamia nuts in the cocktail lounge jog back and forth on the eggshell white sand. Their wives, hailing them from the winding path, beckon them to lunch on the patio. Off near the horizon, a 58-foot sloop-rigged catamaran called the *Mauna Kea Kai* bobs like a prop in an episode of "Hawaii Five-O." Spying the boat, two teenage Californians debate whether or not their parents will let them go out snorkeling on it again tomorrow. The black coral, they explain to a newcomer, is the best they've ever seen, not to mention the colored parrotfish (*uhu* to the natives). "There's even a helicopter that went down in those waters," reports one of the boys. "Yeah, and gold doubloons," cracks his friend. (Actually, the former is said to be down there, but not the latter.)

195

Each floor has its own lobby, such as this one with an Indian storage chest.

In the late afternoon, as the tropical sun inches toward the Pacific, the guests gather for something rummy and for a "pupu," little skewers of pineapple, sausage, and other edibles grilled on tabletop braziers. Later, over a candlelight dinner in a dining room filled with art, two Frenchwomen discuss the merits of visiting Mauna Kea over the Riviera. Their spouses debate whether to golf the next day or visit the volcano. After the finger bowls, they will drift down to a lighted promontory overlooking the surf. There, the nightly action is watching the manta rays flipping like giant butterflies in the water. A few gambling sorts even take bets on the number of flips. The winner buys the next round of mai tais.

Years ago, long before there were mai tais in paradise, Mark Twain visited the Big Island and came home with these words: "Ye weary ones that are sick of the labor and care, and the bewildering turmoil of the great world and sigh for a land where ye may fold your tired hands and slumber your lives peacefully away, pack your carpet sacks and go. A week here ought to cure the saddest of you all."

Kamuela
Hawaii   96743

Telephone
808-882-7222

On the Premises: The sounds at Mauna Kea are of waves and rustling palms, not televisions or radios, which are noticeably absent from the rooms. It was planned as the ultimate getaway, a place where executives could unwind. The hotel has a par-72 golf course designed by Robert Trent Jones, a 13-acre tennis park with nine courts, swimming, sailing, snorkeling, and deep-sea fishing (including superb marlin fishing). The hotel can arrange horseback riding. Hunting for pheasant, wild turkey, boar, goat, and bighorn sheep is possible on the nearby Parker Ranch. For tamer pursuits, the resort offers art tours, lei making, dancercise and water-exercise classes, tennis clinics, and movies.

Rooms: Mauna Kea accommodations are fairly uniform, with the exception of the view. (Seaside is tops.) Each room has a private lanai or porch. The furnishings are casual yet stylish; the chairs are natural willow; the bedspreads are nubby cotton the color of ripe papaya; the walls are covered with bold Hawaiian prints; the floors are laid with cool ceramic tiles; the doors sliding open onto the lanai are teak, as is the built-in dressing-room area and the cabinets in the bath. This is the kind of hotel where the soap is changed morning and night and the toilet paper is sometimes folded into a triangle at the end.

Meals: The celebrated Mauna Kea French toast, a puffy, cakelike concoction, is well worth the calories at the start of the day. The breakfast menu also includes wonderful island fruits, eggs, pancakes, even *mahimahi* (local dolphinfish) and broiled Parker Ranch steak. Lunch at the hotel can be a salad or sandwich by the beach, or the elaborate daily buffet. At dinnertime, guests can choose between three restaurants, each lavishly decorated with art and antiques. In the Garden and Dining pavilions, one can order a full-course meal from a foreign land (Tahiti one night, England the next, Mexico the night after) or choose from the regular Continental menu that shifts nightly. In the third restaurant, the Batik Room, guests may order from a regular table d'hôte menu or a grander a la carte one that offers Burgundy snails, flambéed crab legs, tiger prawns, Pacific lobster tails, deviled rack of lamb and other delicacies. (The hotel permits a certain allowance to its modified American plan guests; after that, the Batik Room charges are on you.) On Tuesdays there is a traditional luau at a waterside point; the menu includes *huli huli* (spit-roasted pig), chicken with taro leaves, *lomi lomi* (salted salmon), salt pork and butterfish wrapped in taro greens, baked bananas and breadfruit, *poi* (pounded taro

197

root), and *haupia*, a traditional Hawaiian dessert made from coconut milk.

Getting There: The major airport on the island of Hawaii is in the city of Hilo, about 90 minutes from Mauna Kea. The smaller Kona and Keahole airports are both less than 45 minutes away. Pickup service is available.

Money Matters: The Mauna Kea is a modified American plan hotel and charges between $230 and $300 per double room, per day; suites range from $300 to $650. Credit cards are not accepted.

Side Trips: Hawaii is still seething with volcanic activity, and lucky visitors might actually witness an eruption in Hawaii Volcanoes National Park. In quiet times, they can drive their car up Kilauea (known as the drive-in volcano) and sip drinks in the historic hotel on the lip of its crater. Hawaii also offers the

tourist lush landscapes of waterfalls, coffee plantations, and picturesque small towns. Historic Kona is the birthplace of the great King Kamehameha I.

Observations: Mauna Kea is a highly sophisticated resort that attracts seasoned travelers with refined tastes and a need to get away from it all. There is nothing flashy or brash about this resort. It is, as they say, quality through and through. Its guests, including many Californians, Texans, and Easterners, return year after year, often with their families. In fact, the hotel has a complimentary children's program from 9 A.M. to 8 P.M. during the busy summer season. Remember that despite the shorts and beach clothes on display during the day, this is a fairly dressy place at night (jackets for the men, although no ties, and designer dresses and pant outfits for the women).

198

**Mauna Kea
Beach Hotel**

What It Costs

"If you have to ask the price, you can't aford it," goes the saying. Unquestionably, many of the hotels in this book are unaffordable by normal vacation standards. But what's wrong with a splurge? After all, there are once-in-a-lifetime experiences to be had at many of these dream getaways. There are also a few bargains if one is willing to go off-season or perhaps take a room minus the ambience or the view. Carefully question the reservations manager and you may be pleasantly surprised. Also ask if there are any special packages available on weekends or holidays.

The following price guide provides average peak-season rates in double accommodations. Keep in mind that peak season varies widely. In Florida, southern California, and much of the Southwest, it means mid-December to late April or early May. In the northern tier, summers are prime time. More temperate areas of the nation, such as Virginia, West Virginia, Georgia, New Mexico, and Colorado, attract crowds year round, with summer generally busiest. In Utah, ski season is clearly peak. Hawaii has become a year-round resort, with the largest number of visitors arriving in summer and at Christmastime.

In calculating prices for the future, don't forget inflation. Hotels tend to raise their prices approximately 10 percent per year.

The entrance to the Ingleside Inn and Melvyn's restaurant, in Palm Springs, California.

American Plan Hotels, Offering a Full Three Meals Per Day

The Bishop's Lodge: $145 to $212 per double room in the summer months; the lodge operates on the European plan in March, April, and May and from September 6 to the end of October, when it closes for the winter.

Black Point Inn: $70 to $95 per person, per day.

The Cloister: rooms average about $100 per person, per day.

The Golden Door: $2,500 per person for a one-week stay.

The Homestead: $96 to $213 per person, per day.

The Point: the price of a room ranges from $200 to $450 per night, including a round-the-clock open bar.

Tall Timber: during July, August, and September, only stays of a week or more are allowed, with the price at $720 per person; in May and early June and later in the fall, shorter stays are permitted at the rate of $150 per person, per night.

Modified American Plan Hotels, Offering Breakfast and Dinner

The Boca Raton Hotel and Club: $205 to $315 per room, per day. (A full American plan and a European plan are also available with rates on request.)

The Breakers: $165 to $245 per room, per day. (A European plan is available in the summer.)

The Grand Hotel: $82.50 to $110 per person, per day.

The Greenbrier: $94 to $123 per person, per day.

Mauna Kea Beach Hotel: $230 to $300 per room, per day.

201

The Georgian Dining Room of The Cloister, in Sea Island, Georgia.

European Plan Hotels, No Meals Included

The Arizona Biltmore: $145 to $200 per room. (MAP and AP available on request.)

The Arizona Inn: $74 to $105 per room.

The Broadmoor: $115 to $155 per room.

Deer Valley: $200 to $325 per night for a condominium operated by Deer Valley Lodging; at the Stein Eriksen Lodge, a hotel room begins at $80 and a condo suite can go as high as $525.

Ingleside Inn: doubles begin at $85.

Inn of the Mountain Gods: approximately $95 per room.

Kapalua Bay Hotel: $143 to $183 per room. (MAP available upon request.)

The Mansion on Turtle Creek: $170 to $195 per room.

Rancho Encantado: $95 to $155 per room. (MAP available in November and December.)

Rosario Resort: approximately $77 per room.

Salishan Lodge: $68 to $110 per room.

San Ysidro Ranch: rooms begin at $98 per night and individual cottages begin at $189.

Sonoma Mission Inn: $105 to $175 per room; a five-day spa program (Sunday to Friday) costs $1,800 per person, a three-day (Sunday to Wednesday) program costs $1,100 per person; the weekender (Friday and Saturday) is $275 per person.

202

What It Costs

A guestroom at Rancho Encantado, in Santa Fe, New Mexico.

Bibliography

Books

Amory, Cleveland. *The Last Resorts*. Harper & Row, New York, NY, 1953.

Ashwell, Reg. *Coast Salish, Their Art, Culture, and Legends*. Hancock House Publishers, Seattle, WA, 1978.

Beam, Philip C. *Winslow Homer at Prouts Neck*. Little, Brown & Co., Boston, MA, 1966.

Cottrell, John. *Laurence Olivier*. Prentice-Hall, Inc., Englewood Cliffs, NJ, 1975.

De Sormo, Maitland C. *Summers on the Saranac*. The George Little Press, Inc., Burlington, VT, 1980.

Flexner, James Thomas, and the Editors of Time-Life Books. *The World of Winslow Homer. 1836–1910*. Time Inc., New York, NY, 1966. Reprinted 1975.

Heinz, Thomas A. *Frank Lloyd Wright*. St. Martin's Press, New York, NY, 1982.

Hepburn, Andrew. *Great Resorts of North America*. Doubleday & Co., New York, NY, 1965.

Ingalls, Fay. *The Valley Road. The Story of the Virginia Hot Springs*. The World Publishing Company, Cleveland, OH, 1949.

Kramer, J. J. *The Last of the Grand Hotels*. Van Nostrand Reinhold Company, New York, NY, 1978.

Martin, Harold H. *This Happy Isle, the Story of Sea Island and the Cloister*. The Sea Island Company, Sea Island, GA, 1978.

McGinty, Brian. *The Palace Inns*. Stackpole Books, Harrisburg, PA, 1978.

Osterwald, Doris B. *Cinders & Smoke*. Golden Bell Press, Denver, CO, 1981.

Porter, Phil. *View From the Veranda. The History and Architecture of the Summer Cottages on Mackinac Island*. Mackinac Island State Park Commission, 1981.

Sleicher, Charles Albert. *The Adirondacks: American Playground*. Exposition Press, New York, NY, 1960.

Sprague, Marshall. *Newport in the Rockies*. Sage Books/Swallow Press, Chicago, IL, 1980.

Vanstory, Burnette. *Georgia's Land of the Golden Isles*. The University of Georgia Press, Athens, GA, 1956, 1970, 1981.

Wessels, William L. *Adirondack Profiles*. Adirondacks Resort Press, Lake George, NY, 1961.

Sources

Pamphlets, Brochures, Periodicals, and Other Sources

Bowdoin College Museum of Art. *Winslow Homer at Prouts Neck*. An Exhibition Catalogue. The President and Trustee of Bowdoin College, Brunswick, ME, 1966.

Carlson, Glenn and Mildred. *The Rosario Story, Orcas Island*. Alexander Printing Company, Everett, WA, 1967 (fourth edition, 1979).

Cohen, Dr. Michael. *The Homestead Zander Collection*. 1980.

Conte, Dr. Robert S. *Nineteenth Century Travel Accounts*. Reprinted from *West Virginia History*, spring-summer, 1981.

The Frank Lloyd Wright Foundation. *The Arizona Biltmore Hotel, History and Guide*. 1931, renewed in 1960.

Geiger, Helen, *The Broadmoor Story*. H.B. Hirschfeld Press, 1968; revised 1979.

Gilbert, John. *Sea Island Company 1930–1980. Alfred W. Jones of Sea Island*. The Newcomen Society in North America, 1981.

Ingalls, Fay. *A Journal of the Sojourn of the Axis Diplomats at the Homestead*.

Kinney, Henry. *Once Upon A Time. The Legend of the Boca Raton Hotel & Club*. Arvida Corporation, 1974.

Palm Beach Newspapers. *Palm Beach Life, 75th Anniversary Issue*. 1981.

204

The original Cloister building, circa 1928, in Sea Island, Georgia.

Photo Credits